EDITIONS

ARMENIAN
BULGARIAN
BURMESE (Myanmar)
CHINESE
ENGLISH
  Africa
  Australia
  Chinese/English
  India
  Indonesia
  Japan
  Korean/English
  Korean/English/
   Japanese
  Myanmar
  Philippines
  Sri Lanka
  United Kingdom
  United States
ESTONIAN
FRENCH
GREEK
GUJARATI
HINDI
HUNGARIAN
IBAN/ENGLISH
ILOKANO
INDONESIAN
ITALIAN
JAPANESE
KANNADA
KISWAHILI
KOREAN
MARATHI
NEPALI
NORWEGIAN
ODIA
POLISH
PORTUGUESE
  Africa
  Brazil
  Portugal
RUSSIAN
SINHALA
SPANISH
  Caribbean
  Mexico
  South America
  United States
SWEDISH
TAGALOG
TAMIL
TELUGU
THAI
URDU

THE ROOM

WHERE THE WORLD MEETS TO PRAY

Daniele Och
UK editor

INVITATIONAL
INTERDENOMINATIONAL
INTERNATIONAL

34 LANGUAGES
Multiple formats are available in some languages

BRF Ministries

15 The Chambers, Vineyard
Abingdon OX14 3FE
+44 (0)1865 319700 | brf.org.uk

Bible Reading Fellowship (BRF) is a charity (233280)
and company limited by guarantee (301324),
registered in England and Wales

ISBN 978 1 80039 268 7
All rights reserved

Acknowledgements
Scripture quotations marked with the following abbreviations are taken from the
version shown. Where no abbreviation is given, the quotation is taken from the same
version as the headline reference.

NRSV: The New Revised Standard Version Updated Edition. Copyright © 2021
National Council of Churches of Christ in the United States of America. Used by
permission. All rights reserved worldwide.

NIV: The Holy Bible, New International Version (Anglicised edition) copyright © 1979,
1984, 2011 by Biblica. Used by permission of Hodder & Stoughton Publishers, an
Hachette UK company. All rights reserved. 'NIV' is a registered trademark of Biblica.
UK trademark number 1448790.

CEB: copyright © 2011 by Common English Bible.

KJV: the Authorised Version of the Bible (The King James Bible), the rights in which
are vested in the Crown, are reproduced by permission of the Crown's Patentee,
Cambridge University Press.

ESV: The Holy Bible, English Standard Version, published by HarperCollins
Publishers, © 2001 Crossway Bibles, a division of Good News Publishers. Used by
permission. All rights reserved.

A catalogue record for this book is available from the British Library

Printed and bound in the UK by Zenith Media NP4 0DQ

How to use *The Upper Room*

The Upper Room is ideal in helping us spend a quiet time with God each day. Each daily entry is based on a passage of scripture and is followed by a meditation and prayer. Each person who contributes a meditation seeks to relate their experience of God in a way that will help those who use *The Upper Room* every day.

Here are some guidelines to help you make best use of *The Upper Room*:

1 Read the passage of scripture. It is a good idea to read it more than once, in order to have a fuller understanding of what it is about and what you can learn from it.
2 Read the meditation. How does it relate to your own experience? Can you identify with what the writer has outlined from their own experience or understanding?
3 Pray the written prayer. Think about how you can use it to relate to people you know or situations that need your prayers today.
4 Think about the contributor who has written the meditation. Some users of *The Upper Room* include this person in their prayers for the day.
5 Meditate on the 'Thought for the day' and the 'Prayer focus', perhaps using them again as the focus for prayer or direction for action.

Why is it important to have a daily quiet time? Many people will agree that it is the best way of keeping in touch every day with the God who sustains us and who sends us out to do his will and show his love to the people we encounter each day. Meeting with God in this way reassures us of his presence with us, helps us to discern his will for us and makes us part of his worldwide family of Christian people through our prayers.

I hope that you will be encouraged as you use *The Upper Room* regularly as part of your daily devotions, and that God will richly bless you as you read his word and seek to learn more about him.

Helping to pay it forward

As part of our Living Faith ministry, we're raising funds to give away copies of Bible reading notes and other resources to those who aren't able to access them any other way, working with food banks and chaplaincy services, in prisons, hospitals and care homes. If you've enjoyed and benefited from our resources, would you consider paying it forward to enable others to do so too?

Make a gift at **brf.org.uk/donate**

thank
y♡u
for all your support

Ravens and manna

What does the Lord require of you but to do justice and to love kindness and to walk humbly with your God?
Micah 6:8 (NRSV)

When I was young and feeling sorry for myself – maybe I had been left out of a group, made a bad grade on a test or felt someone had treated me unfairly – my mother would listen to my woes and then she would say, 'When you're feeling sorry for yourself, the best thing is to do something kind for someone else.' Though I would grumble about it, she was always right. That advice has stayed with me, and it has influenced the way I live my life and understand my calling as a follower of Christ.

In this issue, many writers describe challenging situations when hope was hard to hold on to and it was easy to despair. Despite the uncertainty caused by chronic illness, the loss of a job, financial insecurity or grief, these writers held on to hope and found strength through prayer, Bible study and often by showing acts of compassion to others. They remind us that as people of faith, we can be the hands and feet of Christ or the answer to someone's prayer – the manna in the wilderness (see Exodus 16), the ravens who bring food (see 1 Kings 17:1–6).

Showing compassion and care when we are at our most vulnerable requires effort and courage. But when we do, we remind others of God's faithfulness in all seasons, and we also remind ourselves that God will remain faithful to us. May we all find the strength to remember God's faithfulness, to trust the hope that it offers us, and to share that hope with the world through our actions.

Lindsay L. Gray
Editorial director

Australia-English
edition

Writers featured in this issue of *The Upper Room*:
- Bill Gosling (Australia) • Margaret Martin (Australia)
  • Marion Palmer (Australia)

Gifts to the international editions of
The Upper Room help the world meet to pray.
upperroom.org/gift

The editor writes...

'Truly I tell you, unless you change and become like little children, you will never enter the kingdom of heaven.'
Matthew 18:3 (NIV)

In one way, the start of September illustrates the way in which adults and children can see things very differently. For many in the grown-up world, myself included, regimented by the calendar and the northern seasons, September marks the turn towards the ending of another year. But for children and young people, September represents a significant beginning as they face the start of a new school year.

Granted, it's not a great illustration (what about adults in the education system?), nevertheless it occurred to me because, as I read this issue of *The Upper Room*, I noticed that at least a dozen meditations pointed to the same theme – the different perspective on God that children and childhood provide. Some writers relate an experience from their own childhood; others reflect on the wisdom they have learned from a child or young person in their life. In their varying ways, and inspired by different parts of scripture, they point us to one of the more underappreciated and unsettling 'Truly I tell you' statements that Jesus makes: 'Unless you change and become like little children, you will never enter the kingdom of heaven' (Matthew 18:3).

There are, of course, many other themes explored in the meditations in this issue, as with every issue of *The Upper Room*. Regardless of which of those God uses to speak to us, may we, like the child Samuel, have ears to hear and hearts to respond to the Lord's voice (see 1 Samuel 3:1–10).

Daniele Och
UK editor

Among the contributions that explore the theme of childhood is the winner of our recent writing competition, Georgie Tennant (see 7 September). Congratulations to Georgie for the winning entry and also to the runners-up, April McIntyre and Christine Woolgar, whose meditations are also published in this issue (see 10 October and 1 November).

Courage and strength

Read Isaiah 41:8–16

I, the Lord your God, hold your right hand; it is I who say to you,
'Do not fear, I will help you.'
Isaiah 41:13 (NRSV)

When I was 70 years old, my doctor told me that I had a hernia and would have to undergo an operation. Prior to that I had not experienced any health issues. When I was told that I would need an operation, I was very frightened. But my doctor told me there was no alternative.

On the day of the operation, my fear caused my blood pressure to increase. They could not operate until my blood pressure came down, so another patient was taken in for surgery before me. My family members waited and prayed for me. I prayed as well.

Soon I experienced God's presence and felt that God was reminding me that because Jesus suffered and died, he understood my fear. At that time my fear vanished, and my blood pressure was back to normal when they checked it. My operation was successful. Praise be to God.

When we face difficult situations, we can remember that our great God is always with us and will provide us with courage and support. Praying to our living God, we find new hope and strength.

Prayer: *Dear God, thank you for giving us courage during difficult situations. Please provide courage to all those in need. In Jesus' name we pray. Amen.*

Thought for the day: God can help me through any challenge.

Daniel Samuel Christian (Gujarat, India)

Revival

Read Psalm 19:7–11

The Lord's Instruction is perfect, reviving one's very being.
Psalm 19:7 (CEB)

While away on a short trip, I left a potted plant outdoors in the direct heat in an unshaded area. It was a mistake. I returned home to find the plant's once-green leaves now brown and scorched, its soil hard and dry, and its appearance limp and lifeless. Over the following days, I was determined to nurse the plant back to health with water, fresh soil and plenty of shade. To my delight, the plant eventually sprouted a small, green leaf. As more green leaves appeared, the plant experienced a true revival.

Psalm 19 speaks of another revival – one that takes place in our inner-most being. What water and fresh soil are to dry, lifeless plants, the word of the Lord is to the human soul, especially in times of weariness and despair. The psalmist affirms God's word as the source of the soul's revival – the means by which God nourishes it back to a state of health and vitality.

Circumstances can beat down on us like the intense heat on a summer day, and yet in our weariness, we are not left alone. The Lord, our master gardener, nurses our weary souls to health, bringing new life through the words revealed in scripture. God's word offers comfort, peace, hope, assurance, joy, strength – whatever is needed – so that we not only survive life's challenges but also thrive as God's beloved creation.

Prayer: *Dear Lord, thank you for the precious gift of your word. As we meditate on it daily, bring life and vitality to us. Amen.*

Thought for the day: The word of the Lord revives my soul.

Donyale Fraylon (Texas, USA)

Maintaining peace

Read Romans 12:9–21

If it is possible, so far as it depends on you, live peaceably with all.
Romans 12:18 (NRSV)

Every Saturday I go out for dinner with my family. One family member always wants Chinese food, but I enjoy trying different cuisines. It is challenging to pick a restaurant we all enjoy. Instead of arguing, I always suggest we eat at restaurants that serve a variety of foods. This way we can enjoy our time together rather than wasting time arguing.

In his letter to the Romans, Paul stated how important it is for us to maintain good relationships with others, however hard it might be. With God's peace in our hearts, we can find ways to prevent quarrels that only cause enmity. When we open our hearts to the Lord, the Spirit can help us create peace in every disagreement so that small matters don't develop into big matters.

We will still experience conflict, but God's wisdom can help us know how to react. With the help of the Spirit, we can find solutions to our troubles so that we can remain at peace in our relationships and enjoy the beauty of God's love all the time.

Prayer: *Dear Lord, inspire us with your wisdom and peace so that even in difficult moments, we can find serenity and joy in you. Amen.*

Thought for the day: When I dwell in God's peace, my relationships improve.

Kumalawaty Sundari (Jakarta, Indonesia)

Designed for community

Read Genesis 2:15–22

Encourage one another and build each other up, just as in fact you are doing.
1 Thessalonians 5:11 (NIV)

When I was in college, I participated in a volunteer programme in Thailand with a group of 20 other students in which we helped teach English to children in local day-care centres and schools. One weekend our group hiked through a beautiful jungle. At one point we needed to cross a turbulent, four-foot-deep river.

Many of us were hesitant, and when someone in the group attempted to cross, he quickly lost his footing. It was clear that the current was far too strong for us to manoeuvre on our own, so we all linked arms and crossed the river together. When one of us lost our footing, the two people on either side helped them back on their feet. Without one another, we wouldn't have made it across.

While I haven't literally had to hold on to others like this in many years, I have faced challenges since then that I couldn't have endured alone. God didn't design us to go through life on our own; we need others. Jesus himself demonstrated the importance of community through maintaining a close group of disciples. We need God first and foremost, but we need others too – to lean on and allow them to help lift us up.

Prayer: *Dear God, help us to lean on you as we not only lift others up but allow them to lift us up too. Thank you for designing us for community. Amen.*

Thought for the day: I can rely on God and others to help me through turbulent times.

Emily Marszalek (Idaho, USA)

The dust of God's feet

Read Psalm 8:1–9

The Lord hath his way in the whirlwind and in the storm, and the clouds are the dust of his feet.
Nahum 1:3 (KJV)

I was watching the clouds with my grandfather one day, looking for shapes in them. My grandfather asked me, 'Do you know what clouds are?' I thought: *Clouds form when water evaporates*. But before I answered, my grandfather said, 'Clouds are the dust of God's feet', and he explained that this was in the Bible. This gave me a sense of wonder. If the clouds were the dust of God's feet, then it was as if God had passed through wherever I saw a cloud!

I thought about this repeatedly throughout the week. I even found the Bible verse my grandfather referenced. Then on a day filled with anguish and frustration, I went out to the porch of my house, looking for clouds. I felt restored as I watched gigantic clouds pass over my head. That cloudy day no longer seemed so bad – in fact, it felt freeing. 'God has already been here', I repeated to myself as I watched the sky until my neck hurt. The wind carried the clouds away in time, and my anguish went with them. I went back inside feeling grateful and inspired.

Prayer: *Lord God, guide us out of trouble, and help us to see signs of your presence. Thank you for all you do for your servants and for inspiring us in every way. In Jesus' name. Amen.*

Thought for the day: Where will I look for signs of God's presence today?

Maria Clara Madeira D. Paula Ribeiro (Rio de Janeiro, Brazil)

The big picture

Read Isaiah 55:6–11

So is my word that comes from my mouth; it does not return to me empty. Instead, it does what I want, and accomplishes what I intend.
Isaiah 55:11 (CEB)

I was attending the Saturday men's breakfast at the church. The featured speaker was a man who did chalk drawings as he gave a motivational talk. He began with a large, black bedsheet stapled to a wooden frame.

As he worked and talked, it was difficult to see what the drawing was going to be. He seemed to jump from one feature to another without any sort of plan. He would make chalk marks and then smear them and blend them with marks he had previously made. Sometimes he would simply cross out features he had already created.

It occurred to me that God often works in a similar way. God calls each Christ-follower to accomplish different parts of the divine purpose. It may be impossible for us to see where God is headed, how our part is related or even if God is really making any progress!

But just like the artist on that Saturday morning, God knows the ultimate picture and how each of us fits in. We, however, don't need to know God's final work; we will see it fully when we are with our creator in eternity.

Prayer: *Dear Father, help us accomplish the tasks which you have created for us. Amen.*

Thought for the day: I don't have to see the full picture to follow God faithfully.

Jim Fleming (Indiana, USA)

Coming like children

Read Mark 10:13–16

'Anyone who will not receive the kingdom of God like a little child will never enter it.'
Mark 10:15 (NIV)

If you search the internet for the scripture in today's reading, you can find many artists' impressions of the scene, depicting Jesus surrounded by angelic children, dressed in white, sitting still and smiling.

I must admit, my experiences of my own children when they were small were rarely like that! I have a photo of my son, aged 2, screaming on my front doorstep because he didn't want to stay outside but also refused to come in. It was one of the many impossible toddler-conundrums I faced as he grew.

The artists' depictions of Jesus welcoming children make us imagine them as cute, snuggly and quiet. They're not! They're loud and messy. They cry when things aren't right. But they're also authentic, real, not fake or disingenuous. We learn these things as adults to hide our struggles.

So, when Jesus invites us to come to him like children, it's okay to come as children really are – in all our messy, human complexity. We might need to come to him as a crying, roaring, snotty, stomping child if we need to, not a cute, cuddly, socially acceptable one. We might need to throw ourselves into his arms, laying pride and image aside. We might need to allow him to hold, comfort and heal us and replace our anxious thoughts with his and make us whole.

Prayer: *Lord, help us to come to you like a child today. Amen.*

Thought for the day: I will bring my whole self to God like a child today, however messy that may be.

Georgie Tennant (England, United Kingdom)

New life

Read Luke 19:1–10

If anyone is in Christ, the new creation has come: the old has gone, the new is here!
2 Corinthians 5:17 (NIV)

Yesterday was a beautiful, sunny spring day, and I took the opportunity to ride my bike around a lake. One of my favourite parts of such rides is looking at the trees, plants and lovely views. This time I particularly noticed all the new spring leaves and the blossoms on the trees. As I marvelled at this abundant new life, my mind turned to the new life offered to us by our Saviour Jesus Christ.

Zacchaeus experienced this new life in a dramatic way after climbing a tree to see Jesus and having Jesus invite himself to his home. Zacchaeus' experience with Jesus changed his life, leading him to repay his debts to the people he had cheated in the past.

If we follow Jesus' teachings and get to know him as a personal friend and Saviour we, too, can find ourselves transformed and able to live in a new way. Through reading the Bible, prayer and joining in fellowship with other Christians, we also can be equipped to serve God in new ways and to make a difference in our world.

Prayer: *Loving God, draw us closer to you as we seek to follow Jesus. Help us to share with others the new life you offer us all. Amen.*

Thought for the day: Christ offers new life for all people.

Margaret Martin (Australian Capital Territory, Australia)

Filled with God's love

Read Philippians 4:10–20

[God] gives strength to the weary and increases the power of the weak.
Isaiah 40:29 (NIV)

When I was growing up, petrol stations were called 'service stations' or 'filling stations'. When you drove in, an attendant would come out to your car and ask you what you needed. My dad would always answer, 'Fill 'er up!' The attendant would then pump the petrol, check the oil level, check the air in the tyres and clean the windshield. Dad would never let his car get below a half tank of petrol. He said, 'You never know what might happen, and you might end up somewhere without a filling station close by.'

Dad died two years ago. When I pulled into a petrol station recently, recalling his care for his cars made me think about my spiritual health. Do I let my tank get more than half empty before I turn to God for spiritual nourishment? I realised that, at any time of day or night, wherever I am, whenever I'm feeling low, all I have to do is turn to the Lord. God will not only restore my spirit but also supply all my needs (see Philippians 4:19).

Prayer: *O Lord, our God, when we are down and our spirits are empty, remind us to turn to you for hope and strength. Thank you for being our rock and our redeemer. In Jesus' name we pray. Amen.*

Thought for the day: When my spiritual tank is empty, God's love can fill me again.

Michael D. Stinson (Georgia, USA)

Stuck for words

Read Psalm 104:10–18

How many are your works, Lord! In wisdom you made them all; the earth is full of your creatures.
Psalm 104:24 (NIV)

I never thought that I would ever be stuck for words, but as I gazed in awe at the fiery sunset, I was suddenly speechless. Then, as the city streets became clothed in golden light, the magic happened. Thousands of starlings rose into the sky, and their aerial display began.

Tears of emotion stung my eyes as I watched the flock twirl and spin, constantly changing – swirling, dropping, then rising and falling in a rhythmic aerobatic dance.

Then all at once the murmation was over. The flock dropped almost silently on to the rooftops to roost in safety for the night.

For a brief moment in time, I felt as though I had witnessed the hand of God on our town, and I was blessed by it.

Prayer: *For the beauty of the earth, we thank you, Lord. And we pray with the words that Jesus gave us, 'Our Father in heaven, hallowed be your name, your kingdom come, your will be done, on earth as it is in heaven. Give us today our daily bread. And forgive us our debts, as we also have forgiven our debtors. And lead us not into temptation, but deliver us from the evil one' (Matthew 6:9–13). Amen.*

Thought for the day: 'The earth is the Lord's and everything in it' (Psalm 24:1).

Pauline Pullan (England, United Kingdom)

Sitting with sadness

Read Proverbs 25:11–20

Like one who takes away a garment on a cold day, or like vinegar poured on a wound, is one who sings songs to a heavy heart.
Proverbs 25:20 (NIV)

Over the years, I have had people tell me, 'Smile, it can't be that bad!' or 'God doesn't give us more than we can handle.' At times, I've confided in a friend about a problem, only to be reminded that others have it worse. To be honest, I've said and done the same. Pain – our own and others' – makes us deeply uncomfortable, and in offering such words we try to move quickly through the difficult moments.

But God is teaching me to sit with my own grief, pain and anxiety and that of others rather than trying to rush the healing process. Throughout the Bible, we see examples of lament. In the Psalms and in Ecclesiastes, negative emotions are poured out to God. And Jesus did not hesitate to share his fears with his heavenly Father as he faced death on the cross.

The Bible teaches us that the day will come when God will wipe away every tear (see Revelation 21:4) and turn our mourning into dancing (see Psalm 30:11). In the meantime, as we look with hope towards that future, we can be honest with ourselves and others about what we're going through. So the next time a friend confides in me, instead of saying 'God never gives us more than we can handle', I'm just going to sit and listen.

Prayer: *Heavenly Father, help us to listen to those who are hurting without trying to minimise their pain. Remind us that healing will come in your perfect timing. Amen.*

Thought for the day: I will take time to listen to those who are hurting.

Jillian Bell (Ontario, Canada)

PRAYER FOCUS: TO BE AN EMPATHETIC LISTENER

Guiding light

Read John 1:1–9

You were once darkness, but now you are light in the Lord. Live as children of light.
Ephesians 5:8 (NIV)

My two cats, Jasper and Monica, love to sleep on my bed. It is a warm place, and they feel reassured knowing I'm nearby. But some evenings Monica will fall asleep in some other room of the house and miss bedtime altogether. She will awaken in the dark of night and not know where she is or how to find me. So she calls out pitifully for me to rescue her. Often she is nowhere to be seen, backed into a corner or stuck under furniture. But I don't need to find her; I turn on the light in each room just long enough for her to find her way. Then she joins me, and all is well.

That is a rather silly story, but aren't we all somewhat like Monica? We have a comfortable and reassuring place with God, but sometimes we 'fall asleep' and find ourselves lost. All it takes is a little light from God to guide us. God sent Jesus as the light of the world so that all who believe can find their way to the reassuring presence of God. There are moments when just a little of God's light, reflected through us, can make all the difference for someone.

Prayer: *Ever-present God, thank you for sending Jesus to light our way. May we take every opportunity to show others the light of your love. Amen.*

Thought for the day: Jesus is the source of our power and light.

Tom Ensign (Kansas, USA)

God is our rock

Read Psalm 62:1–8

The Lord is my rock, my fortress and my deliverer; my God is my rock in whom I take refuge, my shield and the horn of my salvation, my stronghold.
Psalm 18:2 (NIV)

Throughout scripture, God's steadfast presence is compared to a rock. This image has stuck with me through the years and was particularly meaningful to me when my sister experienced several bouts of cancer over multiple years.

During that time, I supported my sister from afar by sending her rocks to hold on to as reminders of God's love as she faced numerous tests, treatments and surgeries. Those ordinary rocks served as tangible reminders of God's steadfast love in some of her most trying times. Over the years, she acquired quite a collection, and she always kept a few rocks in her pocket during anxiety-producing tests.

This practice of sharing rocks as reminders of God's love and for encouragement was quite meaningful for us. Sometimes it only takes something small like a rock to lift someone's spirits or to provide loving care. The symbol of the rock can be for all of us a reminder of God's steadfast, comforting presence.

Prayer: *Loving God, you are our refuge and stronghold in good times and bad. Help us to reach out to others in ways that remind them of your strength and love. Amen.*

Thought for the day: I can find strength knowing that God is my Rock.

Mary Hayes Jackson (Texas, USA)

Bruised reed

Read Isaiah 42:1–4

A bruised reed he will not break, and a smouldering wick he will not snuff out, till he has brought justice through to victory.
Matthew 12:20 (NIV)

Last year during the monsoon season we planted drumstick moringa near our house. The plant began growing nicely. With many green leaves it soon reached a height of two feet. I was so happy, and I hoped that it would grow up fast and become a tree. But one day I saw that the plant had been crushed. I didn't know what happened and felt a deep sadness. I felt sure it would never grow again.

But this year during the monsoon season, I was astonished to see that a moringa plant had appeared again in the same place. It was growing again! I thought about how wonderfully the Lord Almighty created the whole of nature. The fact that this plant was growing again was all the Lord's doing. How amazing!

The same is true for humankind. God can restore us when we are broken by grief, anxiety, fear, disease or sin. God offers new life, promising that 'a bruised reed he will not break, and a smouldering wick he will not snuff out, till he has brought justice through to victory'.

Prayer: *Holy Lord, thank you for your promise of eternal life. In Jesus Christ's holy name we pray. Amen.*

Thought for the day: The Lord Almighty can restore my life.

K.D. Macwan (Gujarat, India)

Going interactive

Read 1 Corinthians 12:4–11

When you come together, each of you has a hymn, or a word of instruction, a revelation, a tongue or an interpretation.
1 Corinthians 14:26 (NIV)

A few months ago, while I was working on an idea for a sermon on the apostle Paul, I came across his advice to members of his church at Corinth. How interesting it would be, I thought, if rather than a conventional sermon, the whole gathering was invited to share their thoughts and experiences! When I suggested it to our small but vibrant congregation, they agreed wholeheartedly.

One of our early 'sharing' services had 'A journey' as its theme. Our first contributor explained that his journey of faith had really begun at the age of 18. After suffering from severe eczema for many years, he had as a last resort been taken to see a faith-healer, who had effected a complete and permanent cure for him.

Another item was a journey of discovery made by someone who had researched the background of one of our best-loved Welsh hymns, 'Calon lân'.

Next, one of the congregants shared a story of a journey to the Holy Land. She described gazing in awe at the view from Mt Nebo, and how the trip had brought the Bible stories to life for her and strengthened her faith.

Sharing our faith in this way has definitely drawn our fellowship closer together, and our interactive format is now firmly on our annual chapel services schedule.

Prayer: *Thank you God for the blessing of sharing our ideas and experiences in an honest and informal way. Amen.*

Thought for the day: Are there new ways of worship and sharing God's word that I can try?

D. Carole Wilsher (Wales, United Kingdom)

God's voice

Read Psalm 29:3-9

The voice of the Lord is powerful; the voice of the Lord is majestic.
Psalm 29:4 (NIV)

As part of my fitness programme, I try to walk at least two miles each day around my neighbourhood. When I first started, I would listen to music through my earphones. One day I decided to remove them and just enjoy the beauty of God's creation. I began to notice different types of trees and flowering plants in my neighbours' yards. I also saw different kinds of birds and the occasional deer.

As I approached the end of my walk, I entered the alcove of my front door. Then I heard a bird whose song sounded to me like it was saying, 'Hear me! Hear me!'

As I thought about the bird's song, I decided it was a reminder to listen for God. God can speak to us in many ways – through nature, a friend or even a stranger. It may not be a direct conversation, but if we are willing to pay attention, we might just encounter God.

Prayer: *Dear Lord, help us to seek and receive your guidance. We pray in the name of your Son, our Lord and Saviour, Jesus Christ. Amen.*

Thought for the day: I will be open to what God is saying to me today.

Ellis Smith (Alabama, USA)

Just enough

Read Matthew 6:25–34

Do not worry, saying, 'What shall we eat?' or 'What shall we drink?' or 'What shall we wear?' For the pagans run after all these things, and your heavenly Father knows that you need them.
Matthew 6:31–32 (NIV)

When it comes to work and finances, I have always worried about not having enough. In my early 20s I developed chronic fatigue syndrome, and since then I have never managed full-time work. But I have always had just enough money to get by as a freelance writer. When I complete a project, I often have an anxious voice in my head that wonders, *What if I don't get another one?* Yet the next one always comes.

These words from Matthew 6 remind me that I need to replace that anxious voice with the assurance that God will always provide. What seems miraculous to me is that there is always just enough; it feels like God has a hand in every situation.

I recently became a Christian. Before that, I was tempted by the idea that I could become rich by positive thinking. Yet I never did discover my dream life. When I became a Christian, I realised that what I really wanted wasn't riches; I simply wanted to be safe. I was humbled, feeling gratitude for what I had. God had provided for me all this time, even when I hadn't believed in God.

Prayer: *O heavenly Father, forgive us for our greed and doubt in your provision for us. Please receive our humble thanks for all that you have given us. Amen.*

Thought for the day: When I worry, I will remember that God provides.

Kate Orson (Tuscany, Italy)

Grounded in God's grace

Read Ephesians 3:14–19

I pray that… Christ may dwell in your hearts through faith, as you are being rooted and grounded in love.
Ephesians 3:16–17 (NRSV)

It had been a long time since I operated my model trains. One by one I started the three trains, but at a certain stretch of track, each one came to a complete stop. Because each engine was in good repair, I knew there must be a power-supply problem. The electrical current designed to operate the engines had been disrupted. In order to correct the problem, I had to clean the tracks so that the engines could maintain contact with the track and receive the needed supply of electrical current.

This process reminded me of our need to stay grounded in God's grace. We remain grounded in God's grace by not allowing anything to get between us and God, so that our connection with God remains uninterrupted. Just as I must take time to clean the train tracks, I must take time to cultivate and restore my connection with God.

When our connection to God is broken, we are diminished. The most powerful way to reconnect with the Spirit is through prayer. Indeed, daily prayer is our lifeline to God's life-preserving grace.

Prayer: *God of the ages, keep us grounded in your grace so that we do not lose our connection to you. Sustain us on our journey. Amen.*

Thought for the day: Prayer is my spiritual life's power supply.

Ernest S. Lyght (New Jersey, USA)

God with us

Read Mark 4:35–40

I am always with you; you hold me by my right hand.
Psalm 73:23 (NIV)

I was riding a bus along a twisting highway between cities. The bus bounced and swayed more than usual, and I didn't feel well. As I tried to pray and hoped that I wouldn't throw up, I remembered that in Spanish the same word is used for being carsick and seasick (*mareos*, from *mar*, the 'sea'). I thought of the disciples in the boat with Jesus when a storm arose on the Sea of Galilee. They were frightened – and perhaps seasick – so they woke up Jesus, who was somehow sleeping through it all. 'Don't you care if we drown?' they cried. And he promptly calmed the storm.

What strikes me is that, though Jesus had the power to calm the storm and obligingly did so when they asked, he was already in the boat with the disciples. God is with us all the time – in the storms of life and on calm sunny days. God holds us by the hand in every moment and is ready to answer when we call for reassurance. When we trust in God's loving presence, peace can fill our souls, even in the most difficult times.

Prayer: *Thank you, God, for being ready to answer when we call. Help us to trust in your continual presence. Amen.*

Thought for the day: Jesus is already in the boat with me.

Sister Confianza del Señor (Colón, Honduras)

God's got this!

Read Hebrews 11:1–16

Faith is the assurance of things hoped for, the conviction of things not seen.

Hebrews 11:1 (NRSV)

Five years ago, my husband of 26 years unexpectedly passed away. He was also the father of our three daughters and the primary wage-earner. Now when I think back on those dark days, I can see how I have been in God's hands all along.

I prayed for my broken heart, and God gave me comfort. I prayed for guidance, and God led me to a job that would sustain me and give me purpose. I prayed for my girls, and God has led them along their own journeys. I prayed for help with having two mortgages on our family home, and God showed me how to eventually sell that house and move somewhere much more manageable. I continued to pray for direction, and God introduced me to the man who would later become my fiancé.

I do not need to doubt or fear any new hurdle. I've seen time and time again that God is in control. It's easy to go back to worry when the path is unclear. But I know the Lord is with me every step I take. When I start to fret, I remind myself of what I've been through and take a deep breath. God's got this!

Prayer: *Dear Heavenly Father, even if we don't see the answers we are looking for, help us remember your promise never to leave or forsake us. Amen.*

Thought for the day: I don't need to worry, because I know I'm in God's hands.

Heidi Efta (Florida, USA)

Inspiring faith

Read Luke 18:15–17

'Truly I tell you, whoever does not receive the kingdom of God as a little child will never enter it.'
Luke 18:17 (NRSV)

I like to listen to and learn from children and young people. Many times a young person has challenged and deepened my faith.

A few days ago, I went to visit a family. I noticed their teenager drawing beautiful pictures, and she showed me one of her paintings. Enchanted, I encouraged her to continue dedicating herself to art. Innocently I said, 'Who knows, one day you may go to an art college and learn more about this skill that you appear to like so much.' She promptly answered me, 'Pastor, I will. I pray to God for this, and I know that God will answer me.'

After this conversation, my faith was even stronger. Her response reminded me once again that God's action is realised by faith and trust and that God is attentive to the prayers of young people.

Prayer: *We thank you, Lord, for the examples of faith, trust and praise that young people provide. Help us to follow these examples. We pray as Jesus taught us, 'Our Father in heaven, hallowed be your name, your kingdom come, your will be done, on earth as it is in heaven. Give us today our daily bread. And forgive us our debts, as we also have forgiven our debtors. And lead us not into temptation, but deliver us from the evil one' (Matthew 6:9–13, NIV). Amen.*

Thought for the day: I can learn about faith by listening to young people.

Patrícia Marques (Central Region, Portugal)

The unseen hand

Read Colossians 1:15–17
[Christ] is before all things, and in him all things hold together.
Colossians 1:17 (NIV)

One day in the park I noticed a leaf dancing freely in the air. The leaf would rise to about seven feet, flit about and glide down within inches of the ground. Then it would hover and bob for several minutes as if moved by an unseen hand. This went on for over an hour. I knew it must be suspended by a spider web, but I could not see it.

Watching this leaf reminded me that when Christ went back to heaven, he sent us the Holy Spirit. The Spirit gives us comfort and strength and helps us to choose God's path.

When I feel as if the world has taken control of my life, I have to trust in the one who holds all things in place – God, the creator. The apostle Paul tells us, 'We fix our eyes not on what is seen, but on what is unseen, since what is seen is temporary, but what is unseen is eternal' (2 Corinthians 4:18). No, I cannot see God; I cannot reach out and touch God. But God's Holy Spirit can dwell with us, lifting our spirits and bringing us life.

Prayer: *Heavenly Father, help us to trust you, even when we cannot see where you are leading us. Amen.*

Thought for the day: The Holy Spirit comforts me and guides me on my way.

Sam Whatley (Alabama, USA)

Encouraged at every step

Read Psalm 27:1–6

Wait for the Lord; be strong and take heart and wait for the Lord.
Psalm 27:14 (NIV)

My home is Ukraine, but now I live in Estonia. My friends and I still remember the horror we experienced during the first weeks of the war. We hid in the cellar of a high-rise building for ten days during the air raids. Then we decided to start a long journey out of the country. We travelled through Romania, Hungary and other countries to get to Estonia. Everywhere we journeyed we were met by people who helped us in countless ways. With God's help we found our way out of danger and were encouraged by God's Spirit at every step.

Once in Estonia, I decided together with my friends to get involved as a volunteer, helping to feed the refugees who were fleeing Ukraine. I find that the best way to deal with worries and haunting memories is to help other people. God has been good to us, and in turn we have tried to be good to God's people.

Prayer: *Dear Lord, thank you for guiding us and walking with us always. Thank you for all the friends you send into our lives. Amen.*

Thought for the day: Sometimes God uses strangers to send us the help we need.

Anna Temchenko (Kyiv, Ukraine)

Power of the Holy Spirit

Read 1 Corinthians 2:1–16

I stood in front of you with weakness, fear, and a lot of shaking. My message and my preaching weren't presented with convincing wise words but with a demonstration of the Spirit and of power.
1 Corinthians 2:3–4 (CEB)

I spent most of my life being painfully shy and terrified of taking risks. So several years ago, when God called me to be a Bible teacher, I resisted and refused to use my spiritual gift. I wrestled with insecurities and feelings of inadequacy. The thought of stepping out of my comfort zone made my stomach clench with severe anxiety.

God has brought me a long way by demonstrating that God can give me the words to speak and the grace to obey despite my inner turmoil. Opportunities that would have terrified me before don't intimidate me as much now because God has proven to be faithful. God held my hand as I took small steps of faith and said yes to teaching opportunities. Every time, the Spirit gave me power over my fear and the words to speak.

If God calls us to do something outside our comfort zone, the Holy Spirit will help us. We are vessels for God's glory. We can trust in the power of the Spirit and step out in faith.

Prayer: *Faithful God, remind us to trust in the power of the Spirit within us, and help us to move forward in faith today. In the name of Jesus. Amen.*

Thought for the day: I will trust God and step out of my comfort zone.

Annie McGuire (Missouri, USA)

Belief over fear

Read Mark 5:24, 35–43

Jesus told [Jairus], 'Don't be afraid; just believe.'
Mark 5:36 (NIV)

The waiting room was half full that morning. Many people appeared to be on edge, including me. My symptoms indicated the possibility of a serious diagnosis. I wanted to be emotionally prepared to hear what the doctor might say. As I started to pray, the story of Jairus came to mind.

In Mark 5, Jesus is met by a synagogue leader named Jairus who begs him to come and place his hands on his daughter, who is near death. On the way to his house, messengers arrive saying that his daughter is dead, but Jesus says to Jairus, 'Don't be afraid; just believe.'

Fear can easily overwhelm us when we are faced with dire news. I decided not to let fear control my thoughts and feelings and was determined to give this situation to God. I would trust that God was with me, whatever happened.

Our best response to fear is to trust the God who loves us. When we trust, we fix our eyes on Jesus rather than our circumstances. Whether or not our prayers are answered in the way that we hoped, we can choose to follow Jesus' command to Jairus: 'Don't be afraid; just believe.'

Prayer: *Dear Lord, we thank you for being with us, upholding us and comforting us in every situation. Amen.*

Thought for the day: When trials come, I can trust God and release my fear.

John Schliesser (Alabama, USA)

Breath

Read Genesis 2:1–7

Let everything that has breath praise the Lord. Praise the Lord.
Psalm 150:6 (NIV)

On a recent road trip down the eastern coast of our country, we spent many hours on clifftops looking out to sea for a glimpse of humpback whales. These magnificent creatures that were once cruelly hunted have now returned to the warmer waters to give birth to their young. They are not always easy to spot, but the clue is in their first breath emerging from the depths.

I have heard that the sacred name YHWH, if correctly pronounced, sounds like the inhalation and exhalation of breath. This becomes profound when I consider that every living creature in their breathing proclaims the name of God.

From our very first breath to our final one, we are giving expression to the life God first breathed into the dust that became Adam. May we rejoice in the new life and hope we have – breathing deeply as we praise God.

Prayer: *Creator God, thank you that you are always with us. Help us to breathe your name in all circumstances. Amen.*

Thought for the day: Everything that has breath praises God.

Marion Palmer (South Australia, Australia)

God watches over us

Read 1 Kings 17:1–7

My God shall supply all your need according to his riches in glory by Christ Jesus.
Philippians 4:19 (KJV)

Reading about Elijah's ministry and how God sent ravens to bring Elijah bread and meat reminds me of a time in my life when I did not have a home. I was without a job, and I was facing a mental-health challenge at the same time.

One evening I walked to a church and told the security guard that I planned to spend the night on the church steps. He nodded and told me that a lot of people do that. At that moment I heard someone call my name. I recognised a husband and wife from an organisation I used to participate in. They asked me what I was doing. When I told them I was planning to spend the night on the church steps, they responded, 'No, you are not. You are going home with us.' I accepted their offer.

They took me to their home and for the next five years they provided me food, shelter, transportation and friendship. I had several mental-health crises during that time, and they were persistent in their love and care for me. While living with them, I became employed, got a car and found a place to live. Just as God provided for Elijah, I believe that God provided for me by inspiring this couple to open their home and hearts to me.

Prayer: *Holy God, thank you for watching over your children and for the people who follow your leading and do your work in the world. Amen.*

Thought for the day: God's goodness overflows every day.

Mary Williams (California, USA)

Persevere

Read Job 19:23–27

Since we are surrounded by such a great cloud of witnesses, let us throw off everything that hinders and the sin that so easily entangles. And let us run with perseverance the race marked out for us.
Hebrews 12:1 (NIV)

One of the greatest stories of endurance in the Bible is that of Job. Job suffered the loss of his family, possessions and health, but he persevered and revered God through it all.

I recently had the chance to run in my first half-marathon. Even with months of proper training, I found myself drained of energy and low in spirit with several miles to go before the finish line.

As I began to question whether I would have the strength to make it, I remembered today's reading from Hebrews telling us to run with perseverance towards the path set before us, just as Jesus persevered towards the cross.

These words are a powerful reminder for us to remain faithful to God till the very end, despite the many struggles we are bound to experience. I am proud to say that by remembering God's challenge to persevere, I was able to cross the finish line.

Prayer: *Dear God, help us focus on all you have promised, especially during the challenging times. Thank you for your faithfulness to us. Amen.*

Thought for the day: During difficult moments I will remember God's call to persevere.

Andrew Wade (Alabama, USA)

Rooted

Read Genesis 37:12–28

Be rooted and built up in him, be established in faith, and overflow with thanksgiving just as you were taught.
Colossians 2:7 (CEB)

My sister and I love gardening, so we planted a papaya seed. The papaya tree began to grow, but then one day its leaves turned ugly – apparently a pest had attacked it. My father cut off the top half of the tree, but my sister told me not to worry: 'The leaves will sprout again because the tree still has its roots.'

Staying rooted is also important for us. Even though life may be tough, we can survive if we stay rooted in hope. We see an example of this in Joseph's life. He was sold, slandered and imprisoned. It seemed like Joseph's life was over. But we know that he eventually thrived, becoming a great leader in Egypt (see Genesis 41:41). A big reason for Joseph's success was the hope he kept in his heart. He worked hard, trusting that someday God would turn his life around according to his dreams (see Genesis 37:5–9).

Even when life is difficult and problems surround us, like Joseph we can choose to stay rooted in hope. We can trust that God will help us. With God, hope will forever be in our hearts.

Prayer: *Dear Lord, in every situation remind us not to lose hope. Guide us always to trust that you will help us. Amen.*

Thought for the day: Today I will strengthen my hope in the Lord.

Linawati Santoso (East Java, Indonesia)

Path to joy

Read Isaiah 54:4–7

I lift up my eyes to the mountains – where does my help come from?
My help comes from the Lord, the Maker of heaven and earth.
Psalm 121:1–2 (NIV)

Six years ago, I learned that I would become a widow. My husband's diagnosis meant that over time, his simple pleasures – golf, fishing, throwing a ball with a grandchild – would become impossible. We accepted each day as it came, celebrating the good days and comforting each other on the bad ones. The final four months of his life I was his full-time caregiver. It was the hardest thing I have ever done.

My husband's death brought an end to his suffering, and I was grateful for that. But for me, it was the beginning of being alone and missing the man I had shared life with for 49 years. The intensity of my grief surprised me since I had known this loss was coming for several years. This new form of grief filled me with loneliness and a sense of extreme loss.

I discovered, however, that no matter how unhappy I was with my circumstances, I was never alone. Friends were always available and were very supportive. And God comforted me. I turned to scripture and found God's love on every page. I prayed and felt the Holy Spirit beside me. I turned to nature for solace and rediscovered the majesty of God's creation. Gradually, I found the joy that was dwelling within me all along – the joy of knowing Christ as my Saviour.

Prayer: *O God, our comforter, accompany us in our grief. Help us to rejoice in knowing you as our Creator, Lord and Saviour. Amen.*

Thought for the day: I am never alone when I am in God's care.

Debra Ison (Kentucky, USA)

If you have faith

Read Matthew 8:23–27

*'I have told you these things, so that in me you may have peace.
In this world you will have trouble. But take heart! I have overcome
the world.'*
John 16:33 (NIV)

My wife's grandmother Irene was fond of saying, 'If you have your health, you have everything.' Now that I am experiencing various health challenges, I have a better understanding of what she meant. But while being healthy is important, I prefer to say, 'If you have your faith, you can face anything.'

Today's reading from Matthew describes the disciples' fear during an unexpected storm. They awakened Jesus, who calmed the storm and then rebuked the disciples: 'You of little faith, why are you so afraid?' I think Jesus was pointing out that as long as he was with them, they could face anything.

We see evidence of this later as these same disciples went through a dramatic transformation. Infused with the Holy Spirit after being instructed by Jesus, they spread the gospel message near and far, fulfilling the Great Commission (see Matthew 28:16–20). They repeatedly faced persecution and danger. Previously fearful and confused, the disciples now displayed tremendous courage, in some cases even dying for the sake of the gospel message. Their faith in Jesus Christ caused this change.

We will face challenges in our lives, but Jesus is always with us, giving us peace and courage in times of trouble.

Prayer: *Heavenly Father, strengthen our faith and give us 'confidence in what we hope for and assurance about what we do not see' (Hebrews 11:1). Amen.*

Thought for the day: With faith in Christ, I can face anything.

John D. Bown (Minnesota, USA)

Pour out your heart

Read Romans 8:18–27

Trust in him at all times, O people; pour out your heart before him;
God is a refuge for us.
Psalm 62:8 (NRSV)

I used to struggle to pray because I worried that if I didn't pray for some-thing, it wouldn't be taken care of. Whenever I started to pray about one thing, I would suddenly remember another subject that I felt obliged to pray about instead. But as soon as I started on the new topic, I would think of yet another subject to pray for. This went on and on, and I ended up praying about nothing, which made me feel guilty.

I cried out to God in despair, 'Lord, please show me what to do.' The answer came right away: 'What do you have on your heart right now? Just pour it out before me.' I realised I did not have to worry about *all* the things I needed to pray for. I could focus on the *one* thing I had on my heart now and pour it out before God. I learned that I could take my time with each prayer.

When we let God guide us in our prayers, we can trust that God will take care of our concerns – both named and unnamed. My trust is not in my prayers; my trust is in God.

Prayer: *Thank you, Lord, for being our refuge. Thank you for your faithfulness. Help us to ask for and trust your guidance when we pray. In Jesus' name. Amen.*

Thought for the day: God will care for my concerns even if I don't voice them.

Tahina Rajaomaria (Antananarivo, Madagascar)

Other plans

Read Psalm 94:16–19

When I said, 'My foot is slipping', your unfailing love, Lord, supported me.
Psalm 94:18 (NIV)

My professional career had many twists and turns. I climbed the corporate ladder to become an assistant vice president at a bank. I had expected to spend my entire career at that bank, but organisational changes occurred which ended my banking career after 26 years. I then worked for a non-profit organisation, but funding deficiencies there made me leave. I finally retired as a public-school teacher.

It was during all these employment woes that God became most real to me. At no time did I ever feel that God had abandoned me. I could relate to the psalmist's feelings in our scripture for today. Every time I was out of work and interviewing for another position, I thought, *I'm slipping, Lord!* But each time I can say that God was kind and saved me.

No matter our circumstances, when we turn our lives over to God, we can trust that God will see us through and renew our hope.

Prayer: *O Lord, when we face disappointments, encourage us to trust in you. Amen.*

Thought for the day: When I fear disappointment, God gives me new hope.

Rick Schin (Pennsylvania, USA)

Lifelines

Read Jeremiah 29:11–13

'I know the plans I have for you', declares the Lord, 'plans to prosper you and not to harm you, plans to give you hope and a future.'
Jeremiah 29:11 (NIV)

Our twin granddaughter and grandson were born ten weeks early during an emergency procedure. They weighed two pounds, ten ounces and three pounds, respectively. Within hours of their birth, they were transported to the neonatal intensive care unit (NICU) in a larger hospital. Multiple wires and tubes attached to their tiny bodies monitored their vital statistics and helped them breathe and take nourishment. These lifelines kept the twins alive for two months until they could survive on their own.

During this frightening time, I also had lifelines that sustained me. My relatives, friends and church family checked on the babies' progress daily and offered many prayers for them, their parents and the hospital staff. I have never prayed as fervently or as often as I did during those months. I told myself over and over that 'God's got the little bitty babies in his hands.' This thought brought much comfort to my anxious soul.

When we are in a terrifying situation, we may forget to pray or we may turn to prayer as a last resort. But prayer offers us assurance that God is with us, caring for us through it all. God not only wants us to survive; God wants us to thrive!

Prayer: *Healer God, we trust that you have plans for our present and future. Thank you for caring for us and being with us always. Amen.*

Thought for the day: Prayer assures me that God is with me.

Lu Fullilove (Texas, USA)

One step of faith

Read Colossians 1:1–14

How lovely is your dwelling-place, Lord Almighty! My soul yearns, even faints, for the courts of the Lord.
Psalm 84:1–2 (NIV)

My youth was spent in an existential void filled with doubt. I was searching for something and wanted to fill that void by surrounding myself with people and possessions. Paradoxically, the more I searched and the more things I acquired, the emptier I felt. I finally reasoned that the answer to my deep yearning lay in a spiritual awakening, but I resisted: what would people think?

One afternoon I passed by a church that was usually full of people; but that day it was not. In my quest to find answers to my questions, I went in and spent a few minutes there in silent reflection. In those few moments I found the tranquillity and peace of mind that I needed. I came to understand that the fullness of my existence did not depend on things but on a personal relationship with Jesus Christ.

I began to seek out persons of faith to guide me on my spiritual journey, a journey that restored my life and helped me restore relationships with my family. My newfound faith also inspired me to share in loving fellowship with others who were on the same quest. Most important, as I spent time in prayer and Bible study, my spiritual awakening drew me closer to God.

Prayer: *God of hope, remove anything that prevents us from walking in your light. Thank you for the pioneers of faith who show us how to experience the fullness of life in relationship with you. Amen.*

Thought for the day: One step of faith can lead me to fullness of life in God.

Raúl Robledo H. (Valle del Cauca, Colombia)

Close Communion

Read Matthew 23:37–39

'Here I am! I stand at the door and knock. If anyone hears my voice and opens the door, I will come in and eat with that person, and they with me.'

Revelation 3:20 (NIV)

On a recent Sunday morning, as the service was about to begin, I saw a toddler a few rows in front of me curled up tight in the arms of his father. The small child leaned in so close to his father's face that it seemed as though they were breathing the same breath. I could see the love they shared. Then the child pushed closer still and kissed his father's cheek.

This scene made me think about Communion in a new way. Communion is not just about recognising Christ's sacrificial gift or simply confessing our sin and asking for his wonderful grace and forgiveness. It is also about coming in close and feeling the warm presence of Christ as he offers us new life.

Because of this simple demonstration of love between father and child, Communion will now forever bring me closer to Christ's deep, abiding love. Christ desires close communion with us, not just at these special times but each and every day.

Prayer: *In the special times and in our everyday living, O Christ, may we feel your abiding presence breathing new life into us. Amen.*

Thought for the day: I can experience communion with Christ every day.

Sara McColl (South Carolina, USA)

Recognising God's voice

Read 1 Samuel 3:1–10

Eli told Samuel, 'Go and lie down, and if he calls you, say, "Speak, Lord, for your servant is listening." So Samuel went and lay down in his place.'
1 Samuel 3:9 (NIV)

When I first came to prison in 2006, I didn't know anyone here. When we went to meals, the crowded cafeteria would be loud with many voices talking at the same time. It was chaotic. As I talked with the men around me, I became familiar with their individual voices to the point where I could easily identify who called to me in the crowd.

Similarly, I have wondered how I would recognise God's voice when so many emotions, fears, desires and thoughts vie for my attention. But the more I read scripture, the easier it becomes to recognise God's voice. The Bible is God's word – alive and active – and helps us distinguish among our inner voices, the voices of our world and God's voice. Scripture helps us identify God's voice speaking through the Holy Spirit into our hearts and minds.

Now I am able to hear God guiding me day by day – even conversing with me in prayer. I can hear when God calls out to me because I'm attuned and prepared to listen. We can learn to recognise God's voice by familiarising our hearts and minds with scripture – God's word to us.

Prayer: *Dear Father, open our hearts and minds to your word in scripture. In the name of Christ we pray. Amen.*

Thought for the day: Jesus' sheep follow him because they know his voice (see John 10:4).

George T. Wilkerson (Maryland, USA)

Finding hope

Read Deuteronomy 30:11–14

The word is very near to you; it is in your mouth and in your heart so you may obey it.
Deuteronomy 30:14 (NIV)

I have the habit of thinking that hope is in a remote place rather than where the Lord has put me. When my current situation feels hopeless, I think that maybe I'll find hope somewhere in a more beautiful place. But even then, if I go searching, I may not grasp hope.

However, we are assured that we don't need to go searching far and wide for the hope that God freely offers us. In the midst of trials, when we feel there is no hope anywhere, we can read the Bible and talk with God. I often take some time to go to a private, quiet place where I close my eyes, recall some scripture and offer a prayer. God is near to me in those moments, giving me hope and promising me a bright future. As God's servants, there is always hope when we store scripture in our hearts.

Prayer: *God whom we love, we thank you for time to open the Bible and talk to you. When we are in situations that feel hopeless, help us to remember that you are with us as we pray, 'Our Father which art in heaven, Hallowed be thy name. Thy kingdom come. Thy will be done, as in heaven, so in earth. Give us day by day our daily bread. And forgive us our sins; for we also forgive every one that is indebted to us. And lead us not into temptation; but deliver us from evil' (Luke 11:2–4, KJV). Amen.*

Thought for the day: There is always hope in the Lord!

Riko Suzuki (Kanagawa, Japan)

Serving others

Read 1 John 3:16–24

Dear children, let us not love with words or speech but with actions and in truth.
1 John 3:18 (NIV)

On Saturday mornings, I help sort, pack and distribute food to people in need in our community. Grocery stores, bakeries, restaurants and residential facilities set aside food that volunteers pick up daily and deliver to 19 distribution sites throughout the city. Through this programme, hungry people in our town can receive nourishing food with no questions asked. Volunteers are allowed to take a food box for their own families or a neighbour.

Earlier this year my husband had major surgery, and I stopped volunteering so I could care for him. I knew I would miss seeing my friends weekly, but I would also miss the box of food, which was a big help to us living on a fixed income. However, I was surprised and grateful when Jane, another volunteer, brought us a box of groceries every week while my husband was recovering. Her kindness made me realise how important this programme really is.

Life isn't easy for any of us, but we all can ease another person's burden. Today's scripture reminds us that 'we are God's handiwork, created in Christ Jesus to do good works' (Ephesians 2:10). God gives us the privilege of serving one another with whatever skills we have. Each day provides opportunities to invest our time and talent in other people's lives and show Christ's love.

Prayer: *Dear God, open our eyes to see opportunities to serve others. Thank you for giving us willing hearts. Amen.*

Thought for the day: God's generosity inspires me to serve others.

Elizabeth Erlandson (Nebraska, USA)

Trusting

Read John 14:1–6

God is indeed my salvation; I will trust and won't be afraid.
Isaiah 12:2 (CEB)

Piglet eyes me with suspicion and backs away. I reach out but she's wriggling and squealing. Then, at last, I lift her and hold her close.

Piglet is our large, sleek, elderly guinea pig. She used to belong to our granddaughter and has a grey-white coat, a creamy brown face and a single rosette on top. She likes to eat grass in her run on the lawn, whoops wildly for carrot sticks and loves diving into new heaps of hay.

So why does she struggle when I pick her up? Is she frightened? Or is it all a game? Perhaps she still doesn't know me well enough, doesn't trust me, despite my efforts to make her life interesting. But trust is not easy. It only comes by spending time together, day after day: communicating, interacting, playing together.

Perhaps the same is true in our Christian lives. It doesn't matter how much we learn about theology or how many times we go to church, we need to develop a relationship with God through prayer, study and just 'being' together. If we can do this, trust will grow.

To his confused disciples, Jesus said, 'Trust in God. Trust also in me' (John 14:1). He says the same to us in our challenges. Perhaps, as we look to Jesus, even our panic will subside and we'll allow God to lift and hold us close.

Prayer: *Loving God, help us to experience your compassion as we look into the face of Jesus. Help us to trust and not be afraid. Amen.*

Thought for the day: What can I do to develop my relationship with God?

April McIntyre (England, United Kingdom)

Peace lily

Read John 14:23–27

'Peace I leave with you; my peace I give you. I do not give to you as the world gives. Do not let your hearts be troubled and do not be afraid.'
John 14:27 (NIV)

As I sat at my desk, my heart ached from the hurt and disappointment I had been carrying. Resting my chin on my hands, I let out a long sigh. Just then, my attention was drawn to the peace lily blooming beside me, and the words from John 14 quoted above came to mind. I knew that my heart was indeed feeling troubled about many things. I was feeling afraid and overwhelmed, but here in this verse Jesus was reminding me of the peace he offers.

In this passage of scripture, Jesus shared these words to bring comfort to his disciples at the Last Supper. They were about to enter a very troubling time, and knowing what was to come, Jesus promised to leave them peace.

As I gazed again at the blooming plant beside me, its single white spathe rising above a dark green base of leaves, I decided in that moment to surrender my troubles to the Lord, to let go of fear, and to embrace the peace that Jesus offers.

Prayer: *Dear God, help us to surrender our worries to you. Amen.*

Thought for the day: Jesus gives me his peace when I most need it.

Ginette Armoogan (Ontario, Canada)

Message in a puddle

Read James 3:3–12

Everyone should be quick to listen, slow to speak and slow to become angry.
James 1:19 (NIV)

Some years ago, my ministry included selling a Christian newspaper. One day while I was manning the stand for my weekly paper sales, the pavement was covered with many puddles – some shallow, others deep – from the heavy rain during the previous night. Standing in my usual place, I watched the passers-by attempting to keep their feet dry. The reflection of the dark grey sky made the puddles hard to spot, so often people would not notice one and end up with soggy feet.

Like those passing pedestrians, we can at times 'put our foot in it' with our words. They may be words said in anger or retaliation or that are just inappropriate. They may be a joke that is not well received. When words fly out of our mouths, they cannot be retrieved, no matter how many times we say sorry.

The letter of James hits the nail on the head when he says, 'No human being can tame the tongue. It is a restless evil, full of deadly poison' (v. 8). Words can indeed hurt, painfully so. May we, like those passers-by who were careful where they stepped and avoided putting their foot in it, remember to think twice before we speak.

Prayer: *Heavenly Father, you gave us the incredible gift of speech. Remind us Lord to use this gift not harshly, but with wisdom and tenderness. Amen.*

Thought for the day: May my words today be as sweet as honey (see Proverbs 16:24).

John Hauselman (England, United Kingdom)

God always listens

Read Psalm 23:1–6

Yea, though I walk through the valley of the shadow of death,
I will fear no evil: for thou art with me; thy rod and thy staff they
comfort me.
Psalm 23:4 (KJV)

In 1985 my father was suffering from pneumonia. The doctor told me to contact my relatives, but I had no way to reach them. I was young and in my last year of school, and my father was our family's primary income earner. I was unsure what I would do if he did not recover. Late that night, the doctor told me that my father's condition had deteriorated and he might not survive. I was shaken and broken, and I felt alone.

My parents always taught me to trust in the Lord and to pray earnestly, because God listens and answers our prayers. So I knelt by my father's bed, read Psalm 23 and prayed, 'Lord, I am too young and helpless to take care of my family. I love my father, and I know he is very sick. But you are a kind and loving Lord who can do anything. Please give my father five more years to live.'

When I awoke the next morning, my father's condition had improved. He was discharged days later, and he lived for ten more years. I completed my academic degree and started working so I could help support the family and give my father all the comfort I could.

When we pray, God answers us.

Prayer: *Dear God, thank you for listening to all our prayers and for always loving us unconditionally. In Jesus' name. Amen.*

Thought for the day: I will call upon the Lord to help me today.

Ajay Singh (Uttar Pradesh, India)

Just let go

Read Matthew 11:28–30

'Come to me, all you who are weary and burdened, and I will give you rest.'
Matthew 11:28 (NIV)

When my sister and I were younger, we were given a zip line for Christmas, which our father installed between two trees. My sister and I loved our zip line and wanted our cousin to join in on the fun. She was a little nervous at first, but after watching us, she decided to try it. She was doing great until she got closer to the tree at the end. We repeatedly yelled at her to let go, but she held on – hitting the tree and falling backward on to the snow. Thankfully, she was not injured.

At the time, I couldn't understand why she would not simply let go before hitting the tree. I wonder if God ever wants to yell at us to 'just let go' when we try to do everything on our own, carrying things we were never meant to carry alone. God loves us and offers us rest. We can find this rest when we let go of what we're holding and turn it over to the one who can truly give us peace.

Prayer: *Dear Lord, help us turn our burdens over to you. Guide us to the peace that only you can provide. Amen.*

Thought for the day: I find true rest and peace by releasing my burdens to God.

Mandy Varney (Maine, USA)

Teaching the children

Read 2 Timothy 3:14–17

Train children in the way they should go; when they grow old, they won't depart from it.
Proverbs 22:6 (CEB)

Evelyn is my ten-year-old daughter. For a while now, when I sit to compose meditations to send to the editorial office of *El Aposento Alto*, she has sat down beside me. One morning, to my surprise, I found her writing a few paragraphs about our family. When I asked her about it, she said she was composing some meditations she planned to send to the magazine with the hope that children around the world would place God at the centre of their family life and experience the goodness of God.

Today's scripture from Proverbs immediately came to mind. God always surprises me. For a while I had wanted to teach my daughter the ways of God, but I had, to my dismay, found it easier for me to quote that verse rather than put it into practice. But the good Teacher taught me a great lesson. Evelyn watches what I do and does the same. She writes a few lines, checks the scripture verses in her Bible and sits with me while I write and edit my own meditations.

I will continue to let scripture guide me as I seek to train my daughter in the ways of God, remembering that she is watching me.

Prayer: *Inspire us, God, to set a good example by sharing your teachings with our children so that they may gain wisdom and be nurtured in faith. Amen.*

Thought for the day: Children can teach me valuable lessons about God.

Lillian Saldaña Campos (Havana, Cuba)

Strength to move forward

Read Psalm 34:8–18
The Lord is close to the broken-hearted and saves those who are crushed in spirit.
Psalm 34:18 (NIV)

The moon jellyfish is a fascinating animal. As they swim, their wispy tentacles gracefully trail behind their mushroom-shaped body. When a moon jellyfish loses or breaks tentacles due to injury, it cannot regenerate new ones. Instead, it works tirelessly to reorganise and reposition its remaining tentacles so they are symmetrically spaced around its body, allowing the jellyfish to efficiently navigate the water. The jellyfish's muscles contract and relax constantly to rearrange its tentacles, a process that can take days.

I think about the losses I have experienced, and I recognise a parallel with the jellyfish. When a loved one dies, we cannot replace them; their loss might shatter us. But as we grieve, we also gradually heal and adjust. We work to bring back stability in our lives and look for strength to move forward. This process takes time and looks different for each person.

The psalmist reminds us of the promise that God will be close to us in our tragedy and heartbreak. As we navigate our grief, we can ask God to strengthen our spiritual muscles and sustain us on the journey. God provides healing and repair for our brokenness and 'saves those who are crushed in spirit'.

Prayer: *Heavenly Father, when our hearts are broken, help us navigate the waters of grief. Sustain us and give us strength as we adjust to new circumstances. Amen.*

Thought for the day: God will heal my hurt and help me adjust.

Beverly Taylor (Arizona, USA)

God's good purposes

Read Proverbs 3:1–6

We know that in all things God works for the good of those who love him, who have been called according to his purpose.
Romans 8:28 (NIV)

A highway that I use to travel to and from work was upgraded several years ago. Despite the promises of an improved motoring experience and reduced commute times, I felt apprehensive and occasionally frustrated by the roadwork. However, the disruption was worthwhile when the completed project resulted in freely flowing traffic. Another upgrade is now in progress, and I have learned to trust those charged with the planning and execution of the work for the final result, despite present appearances.

God's purposes in our lives, like the roadwork, can appear to be disruptive, inconvenient and unclear. But when we set aside our misgivings and put our trust in God, Romans 8:28 assures us that 'in all things God works for the good of those who love him'. In all circumstances, especially the challenging ones, we can trust that God is working in our lives.

Prayer: *Lord God, help us to trust your work in our lives so that we better reflect you to the world. Amen.*

Thought for the day: Trusting God strengthens my faith.

Bill Gosling (Western Australia, Australia)

Dwelling on blessings

Read Psalm 145:1–16

You have multiplied, O Lord my God, your wondrous deeds and your thoughts towards us; none can compare with you. Were I to proclaim and tell of them, they would be more than can be counted.
Psalm 40:5 (NRSV)

Recently, I decided that every night when I lie down to sleep, I would give thanks for three things I noticed that day. Some days my gratitude is for something as simple as finding what I needed at the grocery store, getting an encouraging text or email, or feeling the warmth of beautiful sunshine. Other times my prayers of gratitude focus on finding the solution to a computer problem I had spent hours working on or rejoicing with a friend who experienced healing. Many nights, my list is far longer than three things! I am realising God's goodness encompasses my day in ways I often did not notice before.

Focusing on God's goodness has boosted my spirit immensely. Sleep often comes much more quickly than before, and I am blessed with peace. I have found that when I go to sleep dwelling on God's blessings, I wake up the same way. What a difference this practice has made in my attitude and feeling of well-being throughout the day!

Prayer: *Gracious God, open our eyes to the wonderful blessings we receive each day. In Jesus' name. Amen.*

Thought for the day: Meditating on God's blessings brings me peace.

Lucinda J. Rollings (Indiana, USA)

Uniquely made

Read 1 Peter 4:7–11

You are the body of Christ, and each one of you is a part of it. And God has placed in the church first of all apostles, second prophets, third teachers, then miracles, then gifts of healing, of helping, of guidance.
1 Corinthians 12:27–28 (NIV)

We have a shelf in our home where we store an assortment of tools. Some are new and others are old. Some require electric power, while simpler hand tools require only arm strength. Together the tools allow us to complete a multitude of projects, ranging from small crafts to home improvements.

These tools remind me how God created each of us as individuals, but made us all in the divine image. God has blessed each of us with specific talents, abilities and strengths to build the kingdom of God on earth. We are better equipped to serve God and others when we pray, meditate, study scripture and worship with other believers in the community of faith.

Just as each tool on our shelf was created for a certain task, we as believers can work together in our churches and communities to build strong relationships. We can support others by showing the love God revealed to us through the life of Jesus Christ. And no matter where we are, God shapes us and guides us towards a life of loving service.

Prayer: *Heavenly Father, guide our words and actions as we work with others in unity to further your kingdom. Amen.*

Thought for the day: God equips me to follow the way of Jesus.

Daniel Bollinger (Missouri, USA)

Looking for God

Read Psalm 34:1–7

Those who look to [the Lord] are radiant; their faces are never covered with shame.
Psalm 34:5 (NIV)

My job vanished suddenly. Though my supervisor had told me, 'You have planted good seed; we appreciate you, so don't lose hope', a shadow covered my heart. I had been struggling with a season of losses: the death of a beloved friend, a missed opportunity to move abroad, an empty nest after our three children had all moved away.

But the Psalms gave me strength; I found myself crying along with them: 'I have come into the deep waters… I am worn out calling for help… My eyes fail, looking for my God' (Psalm 69:2–3). Eventually, though, I read the words above from Psalm 34: 'Those who look to [the Lord] are radiant; their faces are never covered with shame.' I had found God's promise!

So do not lose sight of God's love. When dark thoughts come, ponder the psalmist's words and look for God's presence: in scripture, in prayer, within your spirit, in beautiful friendships, in acts of love and forgiveness. When we see no light ahead, we can trust the psalmist's words; God is right beside us.

Prayer: *Dear God, sometimes it is not easy to rest in your love and care. But we choose to fight against anxiety and sorrow with your help and that of the people who care for us. Keep us safe in difficult times. Amen.*

Thought for the day: Where do I see God?

Annamaria Vanzulli (Lombardy, Italy)

All-embracing love

Read Romans 8:35–39

Who will separate us from the love of Christ? Will affliction or distress or persecution or famine or nakedness or peril or sword?
Romans 8:35 (NRSV)

One day in the grocery store parking lot I heard a young woman singing a song about God. As I listened to her singing, I became fascinated with her voice and how much love she put into each note of the song. When she finished, I walked over to her and asked her why she was singing that particular song. She smiled and said, 'God loves everyone. You won't see one person out here that God doesn't love. That's why I am singing.' Her answer surprised me; yet her words were true. When I left, I looked around at the people in the parking lot and thought of how God loves each one of them.

With so many painful events taking place in the world that divide and dehumanise, it is good for us to take a minute to realise that God loves each person no matter what they may be going through at any given moment.

Prayer: *O God, teach us to love as you do so that we can show love to all people. Amen.*

Thought for the day: Opportunities to show God's love are all around me.

Steven Moore McNeal (North Carolina, USA)

Sudden changes

Read Psalm 4

Cast all your anxiety on [God], because he cares for you.
1 Peter 5:7 (NRSV)

Sometimes sudden events change our routine and our focus. One day I was moving a bed when it landed on my right foot, fracturing my big toe. This injury changed my daily routine. But though I can't do certain things right now, I still insist on attempting them.

As I think about my situation, I can clearly see how God takes care of us and delivers us every day in the face of our thoughtless, hasty and often stubborn actions. While my activity is limited right now due to my fracture, my prayer is that Jesus will teach me to be more attentive, obedient and calm as I seek to trust and surrender my life to the Lord, my Saviour and Protector.

May God help us hear the voice of Jesus who speaks and says, 'Remember, I am with you always, to the end of the age' (Matthew 28:20).

Prayer: *O Lord, guide us through the sudden changes of everyday life. May your light illuminate our steps. We pray as Jesus taught us, 'Our Father which art in heaven, Hallowed be thy name. Thy kingdom come. Thy will be done in earth, as it is in heaven. Give us this day our daily bread. And forgive us our debts, as we forgive our debtors. And lead us not into temptation, but deliver us from evil: For thine is the kingdom, and the power, and the glory, for ever. Amen' (Matthew 6:9–13, KJV). Amen.*

Thought for the day: Even amid life's sudden changes, Jesus offers peace.

Mariluse Helena Maia (Minas Gerais, Brazil)

Consistent practice

Read 1 Thessalonians 5:9–18

Devote yourselves to prayer, keeping alert in it with thanksgiving.
Colossians 4:2 (NRSV)

I enjoy creating art of all kinds, including painting. One of my art teachers said that daily practice is the only way to improve one's painting skills. I found this to be true when I became overwhelmed with personal responsibilities and put away my brushes and paints. When I picked them back up after quite some time, I found it difficult to paint well. It was only after consistent practice that my skills returned.

Likewise, at one time I became distracted by the things of the world and neglected my Bible, along with my faith practices. When I encountered challenges, I found it difficult to work through them. Thankfully, a family member gifted me with a new Bible and a subscription to a devotional booklet. This was a gentle reminder that it was only through consistent practice in getting closer to God that I could – along with our creator – design a better picture for my life.

Many years later, I remain grateful to the wise, thoughtful person who provided me with that reminder. Sometimes it is helpful when we encourage one another to get back into the habit of practising our faith.

Prayer: *Omnipotent God, may we be consistent in practising our faith. Help us to encourage others in their faith as well. Amen.*

Thought for the day: Daily time with God helps me deepen my faith.

Monica A. Andermann (New York, USA)

Looking beyond

Read Luke 9:23–27

Bear one another's burdens, and in this way you will fulfil the law of Christ.

Galatians 6:2 (NRSV)

I felt my faith failing me. God seemed far away, and praying felt futile; I couldn't figure out what was wrong. That Sunday at church I sat down in the pew, opened the bulletin and an offering envelope fell into my lap. It was for earthquake relief in Africa.

That was it! That was the answer I was looking for. God was calling me to look outside myself, to turn my attention to others. I felt God's presence with me in that moment. Out of gratitude to God for showing me a way through my struggle, I stretched my budget and placed an offering into the envelope.

Looking only within ourselves, we can easily lose sight of our place in God's purposes. The apostle Paul told us to bear one another's burdens. In this way, we find the abundant life Jesus promised. We find our true identity as Christians when we care for others.

Prayer: *O Lord, when we get lost within ourselves, remind us to find our identity as Christ-followers in our service to others. Amen.*

Thought for the day: When I look outside myself, God gives me a new perspective.

Thomas Blanton (North Carolina, USA)

Behind the scenes

Read Isaiah 40:27–31

Those who hope in the Lord will renew their strength.
Isaiah 40:31 (NIV)

I had planted some butternut squash seeds. All my other crops were growing but not the squash.

One Sunday afternoon, I had lost all hope for the seeds. That day I was feeling tired and hopeless because I had not attained certain goals for my life. For many years I had cried over my pain and regrets, but I did not want to cry this time. As the sun was setting, I decided to water the seeds one last time. I carried a bucket filled with water and walked towards the garden feeling depressed. As I approached the grounds, lo and behold, the seeds had sprouted.

I was amazed. It had never occurred to me that God was working behind the scenes. Tears flowed down my face like a river. I was filled with joy, gratitude and hope. When I thought all was lost, God was working. When situations arise that take away our joy and leave us hopeless, we can rest assured that there is always hope in God, who renews our strength.

Prayer: *God our Father, when we have lost all hope, strengthen our faith and hope in you. In the name of the Lord Jesus Christ we pray. Amen.*

Thought for the day: What signs of hope is God offering me today?

Bochere Otachi (Nairobi, Kenya)

Imperfect

Read Jeremiah 18:1–6

We have this treasure in clay jars, so that it may be made clear that this extraordinary power belongs to God and does not come from us.
2 Corinthians 4:7 (NRSV)

The mug I had just bought at the local antique mall had several shades of green and featured a pattern that reminded me of dragonflies with outstretched wings. Wide at the base and tapering up to the lip, it was clear to me that it had been crafted by a ceramics artisan. I turned the mug over and found the maker's mark on the bottom. This piece of ceramic ware had been made by a particular craftsperson for a particular purpose – just as God made me. But why was it in a secondhand store? Then I noticed that the handle slanted to the left rather than running straight up and down the side of the mug. It wasn't perfect, but it still held my morning coffee just fine.

The green mug has made me think about my own imperfections. Sometimes I fail to listen with a loving heart. At times I've lost my temper. Scripture says, 'All have sinned and fall short of God's glory' (Romans 3:23, CEB). Yet, I do not lose hope! The Bible reminds us of God's faithful people who, though imperfect, made themselves available to do God's work. Moses, Noah, Rahab, Peter and Paul – none of them was perfect. Their examples remind me that even though I'm imperfect, I can still share God's love with the world and serve God faithfully.

Prayer: *Gracious Creator, thank you for loving us and for using us to spread your love. Help us not to let our imperfections get in the way of serving you and others. Amen.*

Thought for the day: God can use me in spite of my imperfections.

Deborah L. Ormay (Pennsylvania, USA)

Community of faith

Read Exodus 18:5–27

Moses' father-in-law replied, 'What you are doing is not good. You and these people who come to you will only wear yourselves out. The work is too heavy for you; you cannot handle it alone.'
Exodus 18:17–18 (NIV)

Soon after the Israelites' deliverance, Jethro – Moses' father-in-law – came to visit and observed Moses in his daily responsibility of judging disputes between the people. Jethro told Moses that continuing to do all the work alone would be too much. He advised Moses to set wise men as leaders over groups of people. In following this advice, Moses relied on his community for help and prevented his own burnout.

God designed us to need community. It can be uncomfortable and hard to accept that we need others, especially when we realise that our church is made up of imperfect people. But when we downplay the collective nature of our faith, we do ourselves a disservice.

Wonderful things can happen when we rely on each other: our bonds of relationship are strengthened, and we give others the opportunity to show God's love to us. In big and small moments, let's commit to loving those around us and letting others love us in return. In doing so, we can be a part of ushering in God's kingdom.

Prayer: *Dear Lord, thank you for the community of believers. Help us to reach out to others who may need our love, and help us to accept love in return. Amen.*

Thought for the day: My personal faith is lived out in community with others.

Sarah K. Butterfield (California, USA)

Hearing God's voice

Read John 10:1–10

'I am the good shepherd. I know my own sheep and they know me.'
John 10:14 (CEB)

When I was in middle school, my family had many chickens. One day, a mother hen went into the fields outside to feed her chicks and a chick fell into a hole in the ground. When it became dark, the hen returned to our house with her other chicks, leaving the lone chick behind.

After some time, my father heard the chick crying, and he tried to retrieve it from the hole. But the little chick was afraid and did not respond to my father's voice, so he could not get it out. When I saw what was happening, I brought the mother hen to the hole and she called out to the chick. On hearing its mother's voice, the chick immediately came out of the hole.

Today, many years later, I still recall that evening. When the little chick heard its mother's voice, its fear vanished. In the same way, during difficult times we can listen for our heavenly Father's voice. God can deliver us from any situation.

Prayer: *Heavenly Father, help us to listen for your voice and come to you in any situation. In Jesus' name we pray. Amen.*

Thought for the day: God is always speaking to me; I will listen and respond.

Donald Milan Waghela (Gujarat, India)

Refreshing moments

Read Psalm 84:1–9

They go from strength to strength, till each appears before God in Zion.
Psalm 84:7 (NIV)

After dropping my kids off at school and day care one morning, my minivan started smoking. Thankfully, I made it safely to work, but I fretted about what might be wrong with the minivan. Would it be safe enough to pick up my kids in after school? I was going through a difficult time in my life – divorce, financial challenges, health issues, the basement flooding – and this just felt like another thing spiralling out of my control. As I sat there feeling incredibly hopeless, a friend called to check on me. I told her about the minivan, and she prayed with me.

In the end, I was able to pick up my kids and drive home that day, but the minivan wasn't repairable. Even so, knowing I had a friend walking through this time with me, someone praying with me, was like coming upon a refreshing pool during a long, difficult journey.

Similarly, the people in Psalm 84 found springs and pools of rain when they passed through the Valley of Baka. God provided refreshing moments for them along the way to sustain them on the journey. God shows up for us in such creative and timely ways through people, words, nature and in other ways we could not even imagine.

Prayer: *Dear God, help us to notice and experience the refreshing pools of strength you provide as you walk with us through difficult circumstances. Amen.*

Thought for the day: God will provide refreshing moments to sustain me.

Amanda Gott (Ohio, USA)

PRAYER FOCUS: THOSE WITHOUT RELIABLE TRANSPORTATION

New every morning

Read Lamentations 3:19–24

Because of the Lord's great love we are not consumed, for his compassions never fail. They are new every morning; great is your faithfulness.

Lamentations 3:22–23 (NIV)

I can relate to the writer of Lamentations. Some mornings I wake up to the worry of another difficult day. When I remember my afflictions, my heart sinks and I find myself teetering on the edge of another bout of depression.

However, Lamentations presents a turning point that keeps me from deep hopelessness. When I recall what God has done in the past, I am humbly reminded that God will also sort things out for me. I have faced many tough situations where I could see no way out, but each time God showed me mercy and faithfulness.

God has made me a witness of the promise that through God's mercies I am not consumed. I am still standing, made strong by the grace of God. I know I can hope in God's unfailing compassion because it is new every morning.

Prayer: *Faithful God, thank you for your compassion and mercy. Give us strength when we are weary, and remind us of your constant love. Amen.*

Thought for the day: Even when I am in turmoil, God shows me compassion.

Natalie Su Ting Tan Estee (England, United Kingdom)

Guiding signs

Read Exodus 13:17–22

[God] guided them with the cloud by day and with light from the fire all night.
Psalm 78:14 (NIV)

I like to start my day with a run to clear my mind and to feel refreshed and energised. While I was on a recent early morning run, I was reminded of God's great mercy and protection. As I ran, I happened to glance up at the sky and noticed one particular cloud that seemed to be leading me on. It reminded me of the story of God using a cloud to lead the Israelites on their journey towards the promised land.

I pondered the words from Psalm 78:14 as I finished my run. I believe God reveals to us each day the ways we should go – the ways that are best for us. But are we willing to accept God's leading? The cloud seemingly led me that morning, and I believe God placed it in the sky specifically for me so that I could recall the goodness and grace that God has given me. Such recollections reassure us that God really is providing direction in our lives.

Prayer: *Lead us this day, Father, to the place where you need us to go. Help us to experience you in new ways. We thank you for your direction in our lives. Amen.*

Thought for the day: God's guiding signs are everywhere.

Todd Diedrich (Wisconsin, USA)

Seeking joy

I will be 24 years old by the time you read this, and without question I have lived in unprecedented times – I was two years old when 9/11 occurred; I was a freshman in high school when the Sandy Hook shooting happened; I have witnessed a rise in mass shootings and gun violence. If this were not enough, my college years saw a pandemic and the growing effects of global warming.

As I look back over my childhood, teenage years and young adult life, I take a moment of lament for the world we have created for ourselves and one another. But alongside my lament, I find myself seeking grounding, joy and release. Personally, I struggle with the biblical instruction to 'count it all joy' when we face trials (see James 1:2). Sometimes it is truly impossible to count something as joy, but perhaps we can take a small step towards this by finding tiny moments of joy and centring amid deep sorrow.

The urge to look for joy even in times of deepest sorrow reminds me of Genesis 18:1–14. When Sarah was told she would bear a son, she laughed. Sarah was past childbearing age when angels brought this news to her. It was seemingly impossible, and I can only imagine how preposterous this suggestion must have sounded to her. Maybe Sarah's laughter was grounding for her. Laughing – even at the most inopportune times – can relieve stress, creating a calming and soothing effect. While we may not laugh in difficult moments, welcoming the fullness of our feelings in all circumstances can allow us to process and make space for deeper reflection and discernment.

In moments of shock or tragedy, actions that offer us relief and a sense of being present in our body may be as divine an act as prayer. Such action may look different for all of us, whether it be breathing deeply, crying, laughing out loud, going for a run, dancing around the house with friends or just lying on the living room floor. Whatever the action, finding, creating and welcoming even the smallest moment of grounding may be the first step towards embracing and expressing our feelings and finding our agency in difficult situations.

When we look at Sarah, we are reminded that after her laughter, she gave birth to a son and welcomed what God had promised her. Sarah reminds us that ordinary, daily actions can ground us and help us to embrace the possibilities God puts before us. In the midst of the unprecedented, we can feel our emotions to their fullest. Doing so offers us moments of stillness and opportunities to pray or worship. But then we are called to join with our community and to take action to make our world a better place.

QUESTIONS FOR REFLECTION

1 When you feel untethered or ungrounded, what activities help bring you back into yourself?

2 What parts of your community help you feel most alive and most like yourself?

3 When you think about what grounds you and the parts of your community that make you your best self, how might you draw these two things together to create a space where you and your community can be grounded together? How might that communal grounding be turned into action for the betterment of the world?

Tatayana Richardson

Stay or go?

Read Isaiah 55:8–13

'So is my word that goes out from my mouth: it will not return to me empty.'
Isaiah 55:11 (NRSV)

Over the last 14 years, I have tried – several times – to leave my employer.

At first, it was because I was unhappy. Later, the Holy Spirit prompted me to interview for external roles but I wasn't offered one. Even now, I feel the tug of wondering if here is where I'm meant to be. It's not that I have a bad job or don't generally enjoy what I do; I just don't see myself achieving very much for God's purposes. If I was somewhere else, couldn't I be better utilised?

When I first started with my employer, Isaiah 55:10–11 stood out to me: just as rain doesn't return to the sky without producing crops, neither would I leave this workplace until God had accomplished what God purposed to do through me. I often come back to these verses. What exactly is God's purpose? Will I recognise it? Are we nearly done yet?

The missiologist Christopher Wright wrote: 'I may wonder what kind of mission God has for me, when I should ask what kind of me God wants for his mission.' Following God's call can of course be fulfilling, but utilising my supposed untapped potential isn't the goal. So I remind myself of God's promise: I may not know exactly why I am where I am, but if God won't let me return empty, then I am content.

Prayer: *Lord, help us not to see ourselves in utilitarian terms. Give us patience and enable us to give you joy in both who we are and what we do. Amen.*

Thought for the day: Do I trust God to place me where God wants me?

Christine Woolgar (England, United Kingdom)

Seeds of faith

Read Romans 8:12–17

You didn't receive a spirit of slavery to lead you back again into fear,
but you received a Spirit that shows you are adopted as his children.
With this Spirit, we cry, 'Abba, Father.'
Romans 8:15 (CEB)

My son had been in pain for three months, and when he went in for a scan, it showed that he had a small growth on one of his bones. My quick search of the internet scared me, flooding me with worry that he could end up unable to walk.

But at that moment, the Holy Spirit urged me to pause and remember all the promises of God. In response, I consciously countered my negative thoughts and said to myself, 'My son is going to live a long and healthy life.' When I started repeating these words in my mind, my whole outlook changed. I experienced a feeling like a blanket of peace wrapped around me.

The enemy who comes to steal our joy sows the seed of doubt in our lives which leads to fear. But we must not allow those seeds to grow. When we recognise seeds of doubt and fear, we can pluck them out and replace them with seeds of faith. We can hold fast to the assurance that we 'didn't receive a spirit of slavery to lead [us] back again into fear'. When we receive the Holy Spirit into our hearts, it will lead to new life.

Prayer: *Dear God, deliver us from fear. Help us to trust in your word wholeheartedly and live a life of freedom. Amen.*

Thought for the day: I will fill my mind with the word of God.

Mary Shiny Lijo (Karnataka, India)

Words and actions

Read 1 John 3:11–15

Dear children, let us not love with words or speech but with actions and in truth.
1 John 3:18 (NIV)

A local church uses a renovated movie theatre as their house of worship. Along the roads leading to their parking lot, the church has erected large billboards that proclaim, 'You Belong!' However, the entrances to their parking lot are usually blocked by sturdy padlocked gates.

When I first saw these gates, I felt like they contradicted the message on the billboards. But as I continue to drive by these apparent mixed messages, I have realised that instead of shaking my head at them, my energy would be better spent by looking at my own words and actions. I say I'm a Christian, but do I get angry and think ugly thoughts when I notice distracted drivers? I proclaim that I want to serve others, but do I direct my efforts only towards the people I know and feel most comfortable around? Do those who observe me on my walks see me as joyfully Christ-filled or as gloomily preoccupied with myself?

First John is addressed to a Christian community undergoing a bitter split. First John 3:18 reminded the church then and reminds us now that the love of Christ is authentic love. Let us practise love rather than just talk about it.

Prayer: *Dear Jesus, though we call you Lord, many times our actions do not follow your teachings. Help us to live out our beliefs. Amen.*

Thought for the day: Today I will strive to act in a way that reflects my faith.

Larry V. Jones (North Carolina, USA)

PRAYER FOCUS: TO LIVE OUT MY FAITH   73

A beautiful reminder

Read Psalm 121:1–8

My help comes from the Lord, the Maker of heaven and earth.
Psalm 121:2 (NIV)

As I rounded a corner on the parkway, I was dazzled by the wonderful sight of glistening snow on the Brindabella Mountains. It was a freezing-cold, wintery day in Canberra as I drove to my choir rehearsal. This was to be the last practice before our concert in a week's time. As the choir's events manager, I had many worries and much to accomplish for the rehearsal and concert.

With the mountains in view before me, I thought of Psalm 121: 'I lift up my eyes to the mountains – where does my help come from? My help comes from the Lord, the Maker of heaven and earth.' This beautiful scene was a timely reminder to me of God's presence in my life. It prompted me to pass my concerns over to God in prayer, and as I continued my journey I felt a sense of peace and thankfulness for God's loving-kindness and care. God is near and ready to help if only we ask.

Prayer: *Dear God, thank you for creating a beautiful world that reminds us of your love and care for us. Thank you for hearing our prayers when we bring our worries to you. Amen.*

Thought for the day: I will remember to ask God for help when I need it.

Margaret Martin (Australian Capital Territory, Australia)

The labyrinth

Read Philippians 4:4–9

The peace of God, which transcends all understanding, will guard your hearts and your minds in Christ Jesus.
Philippians 4:7 (NIV)

When my husband of 25 years told me he thought our marriage was over, I was stunned, devastated and afraid. For a few weeks, I walked around in a daze – going through the motions of my life but not really living it.

Shortly after, I had the opportunity to walk a prayer labyrinth, an ancient practice used for centring, contemplation and prayer. This labyrinth was located on a cliff overlooking the ocean.

As I followed the winding path, my senses were awakened. I became aware of God's creation surrounding me. I felt the warmth of the sun, smelled the nearby flowering shrubs and heard waves crashing on the shore below. I brought my devastation and fears to God as I traversed the twists and turns of the labyrinth. When I reached the centre, I surrendered my marriage and entrusted my future to God, who loves me unconditionally.

The peace that overwhelmed my soul when I surrendered my fears to God sustained me through this past year. Fear can leave us struggling to get our bearings, to see a clear path forward. Centring ourselves in Christ gives us an anchor to hold on to and a guide to walk with us through the most challenging times.

Prayer: *Dear God, may we always be aware of your presence with us and turn to you when we are afraid. We long for the peace you have promised through Jesus Christ. Amen.*

Thought for the day: Nothing is too big or too small to surrender to God.

Victoria Kubasak (California, USA)

Tracks to safety

Read Psalm 119:97–105

Your word is a lamp for my feet, a light on my path.
Psalm 119:105 (NIV)

I remember being caught in a snowstorm while driving through a high mountain pass. The snow soon developed into a blizzard, and I was unable to see more than a few feet ahead. But a truck in front of me was leaving tyre tracks in the six-inch deep snow, so I did the only thing I could – I followed the tracks. If the truck had driven off the cliff, I would have been right behind it! Eventually, though, it led me down the mountain to safety.

That experience caused me to remember these words from Psalm 119: 'Your word is a lamp for my feet, a light on my path.' Spiritually speaking, it can be as difficult for us to know the way forward as it was for me to find my way in that snowstorm. Temptations may be intense at times. Or we may simply find ourselves at a fork in the road, unsure of which path to take. No matter the cause, the way forward for us at times may not be clear. But when we rely on the wisdom of Psalm 119, God's word can dispel the darkness and reveal the way we should go. When we are grounded in scripture, God's guidance keeps us ready for any trial.

Prayer: *Dear God, help us to hear your voice speaking to us through scripture, especially in difficult times. Guide us each day and reassure us of your presence with us. Amen.*

Thought for the day: God's wisdom in scripture brings clarity to my confusion.

Awlwyn Balnave (British Columbia, Canada)

Humility

Read Genesis 33:1–11

[Jacob] himself went on ahead and bowed down to the ground seven times as he approached his brother.
Genesis 33:3 (NIV)

As soon as the words left my mouth, I regretted saying them. I shook with anger from our argument, but I knew I needed to apologise to my husband. But I struggled to apologise because of my pride.

In the Bible, Jacob overcame his pride. He had stolen his brother Esau's birth right, and when he saw Esau coming with 400 men, he knew he was in trouble – just like I knew I was in trouble after my argument. So Jacob humbled himself. He bowed seven times, as did his maids, wives and children. They all humbled themselves because they needed mercy.

This story in Genesis reminded me that 'God opposes the proud but gives grace to the humble' (1 Peter 5:5, NRSV). I didn't bow to the ground in front of my husband, but I did bow my heart and put what God wanted above my pride.

Remembering that mending a relationship requires humility can help us overcome our pride. Humility helps us reconcile broken relationships. Let's rely on God's grace to stay humble.

Prayer: *Merciful God, help us to walk in humility and open our hearts to your will for us. Amen.*

Thought for the day: Humility can bring grace and reconciliation into my life.

Lenita Reeves (Maryland, USA)

Peace from prayer

Read 2 Corinthians 1:3–4

*Jesus said, 'Peace I leave with you; my peace I give you. I do not give
to you as the world gives. Do not let your hearts be troubled and do
not be afraid.'*
John 14:27 (NIV)

The months following my cancer diagnosis felt incredibly long. There
were medical appointments, several scans and tests, followed by more
appointments, and then waiting for surgery. One week after surgery, I met
with the surgeon to review results and discuss next steps.

That morning I began my devotion time by reading *The Upper Room*,
a habit I've had for almost 40 years. The writer talked about her anxiety
over an upcoming medical appointment and how she calmed her fears
by thinking about the many friends who were praying for her. Over the
next hour, I received text messages from several friends telling me they
were praying for me that morning.

I have felt remarkable peace going through this process, praise the
Lord! I attribute that to prayers on my behalf and the comfort of knowing
that Jesus walks with me. I've also tried to focus on what God may be
trying to teach me. I am learning a lot about patience, perspective and
perseverance. Most of all, I am reminded daily to trust God, who provides
'the peace… which transcends all understanding' (Philippians 4:7).

Prayer: *Heavenly Father, as we go through challenging times, help us
to put our trust in you. Help us also to remember others in our prayers
and support them as they face difficult situations. Amen.*

Thought for the day: No matter what I face, the prayers of others give
me strength.

John D. Bown (Minnesota, USA)

A special invitation

Read Luke 14:15–24

Jesus said, 'Come to me, all you who are weary and burdened, and I will give you rest.'
Matthew 11:28 (NIV)

'Sister, will you come to my dinner on 24 July?' my friend asked. I had met this friend in a Christian fellowship group in 2019, but I later joined a new group and did not see her much anymore. It took me a moment to remember that her birthday was in July. She was inviting me to be part of the celebration. For me, that was a special and unexpected invitation.

In a similar way, each of us has received a special and perhaps unexpected invitation from Jesus, our Lord. Jesus said, 'Come to me, all you who are weary and burdened.' Thankfully, Jesus' invitation has no deadline. We can come to him at any time, bringing our burdens, frustrations and problems. For those who accept his invitation, Jesus promises rest, healing and comfort.

Just as I immediately and excitedly accepted the invitation to my friend's birthday party, my response to Jesus' invitation is swift and grateful. Everyone who is weary and burdened can accept Jesus' call to lay down their burdens and find rest.

Prayer: *Dear Jesus, thank you for the peace you give us when we respond to your invitation and your promise. Amen.*

Thought for the day: What is Jesus' invitation for me today?

Linawati Santoso (East Java, Indonesia)

A good plan

Read Proverbs 16:1–9

In their hearts humans plan their course, but the Lord establishes their steps.
Proverbs 16:9 (NIV)

As an animal lover, I was ecstatic to apply and interview for a job managing a local veterinary clinic. It was my dream job. The interview with the clinic owner couldn't have gone better. We got along great and discussed the future of the clinic as she gave me a full tour and introduced me to staff.

Although I was convinced this was a perfect fit for me, I asked God for guidance and to either open or close the door to this opportunity according to God's plan. When I found out a week later that I was not selected for the job, I was heartbroken. But I had to remind myself in my disappointment that God had indeed answered my prayer about this decision. I had asked God to open or close the door, and God had done just that.

While I think I know the right course for my life, God always knows best. When we remain humble and submit to God's will, we can be certain that God has a good plan for our lives and can use all things – even disappointments – for good.

Prayer: *Dear God, thank you for directing our steps and reminding us that you have a good plan for our lives. We pray as Jesus taught us, 'Our Father in heaven, hallowed be your name, your kingdom come, your will be done, on earth as it is in heaven. Give us today our daily bread. And forgive us our debts, as we also have forgiven our debtors. And lead us not into temptation, but deliver us from the evil one' (Matthew 6:9–13, NIV). Amen.*

Thought for the day: In each decision I make, I will trust God.

Emily Marszalek (Idaho, USA)

My presence will go with you

Read Exodus 33:12–17

'The Lord bless you and keep you; the Lord make his face shine on you and be gracious to you; the Lord turn his face towards you and give you peace.'

Numbers 6:24–26 (NIV)

The church my sister and I had worshipped in for 34 years was closing after almost 115 years of worship and service, before uniting (happily!) with a local church. Naturally that Sunday morning my feelings were mixed – thanksgiving for all God's goodness and guidance in the past, and sadness at the end of an era in our beautiful sanctuary.

In my morning devotions, I always read five hymns, going through three hymnbooks in turn. Each one has around 700 hymns, so it takes many months to complete. On the morning of the last service, I turned as usual to start reading the first of the next set of five hymns for that day. It turned out to be a hymn based on the Aaronic blessing from Numbers 6, which I knew the congregation were going to be singing to each other after the benediction in a few hours' time. The next hymn was also from the Church of Scotland hymnbook, Church Hymnary 4th edition, with words by Ian Jamieson: 'May the peace of God go with us.'

I truly felt that our almighty and gracious God was reassuring me that he would always be with me, wherever I worship him.

Prayer: *Father, we give you thanks for the faithful service of your people in times past, and know that the future is also in your safe keeping. Be with those who minister to churches which have united, and give grace to us all to love one another in your name. Amen.*

Thought for the day: God's presence is everywhere with his people.

Christine Hay (Scotland, United Kingdom)

God's purpose

Read Jonah 1:1–17

The Lord Almighty has sworn, 'Surely, as I have planned, so it will be, and as I have purposed, so it will happen.'
Isaiah 14:24 (NIV)

It is my fourth year of serving as the student advisor for the Christian Fellowship Society at a women's university in Lahore, Pakistan. Initially when this role was offered to me, I firmly refused. At the time I had an infant and a toddler, not to mention my academic responsibilities.

But God continued to call me to work with young Christian girls at the university. The opportunity to lead the society came to me again, and I was the only person available. This time I felt I had to accept, and I started shortly before the Christmas festival – the society's most anticipated event of the year. With around 100 girls working on it, the Christmas production was a huge success, glorifying Jesus and celebrating his birth.

The way things fell into place was truly divine intervention, and this experience taught me that what God has planned will come to fruition. My calling to this role was much like Jonah's. He tried his best to run away from the task God gave him only to end up in the belly of a huge fish! Like Jonah, no matter how far we run, God will call us back and guide us in the right direction.

Prayer: *Dear Lord, grant us the courage to work according to your will so that our words and actions may glorify you. Amen.*

Thought for the day: When God calls me, I will follow.

Sammar Aaroon (Punjab, Pakistan)

In all circumstances

Read 1 Thessalonians 5:16–24

Give thanks in all circumstances; for this is God's will for you in Christ Jesus.
1 Thessalonians 5:18 (NIV)

A year and a half ago I was diagnosed with breast cancer. In the past I have tried to trust God in all circumstances, but I frequently still hung on to my worries and even wanted to tell God exactly how to fix things. But this time was different. I gave it all to God.

Even though I wanted to be around to see my grandchildren grow into adults and spend more time with my family, I left it in God's loving hands. I didn't ask God for a cure. Instead I asked for God's help in accepting whatever happened with my treatment. No matter what, I was grateful for my time on earth.

I felt profound peace in trusting God and wasn't anxious about the outcome of my treatment. After some time, I found that I was able to give thanks even with my diagnosis. I did not want cancer, nor would I wish it on anyone else. But it helped me to focus on what truly matters. It also taught me greater empathy for others facing serious health issues. I experienced the peace that comes from truly giving my troubles to the Lord.

Prayer: *Loving and compassionate Lord, help us to trust you and give thanks in all circumstances. Amen.*

Thought for the day: I will ask for help and trust God with the outcome.

Julie Breutzmann (Iowa, USA)

PRAYER FOCUS: PEOPLE WITH CANCER

Finishing well

Read 1 Corinthians 9:24–27

Everyone who competes in the games goes into strict training. They do it to get a crown that will not last, but we do it to get a crown that will last forever.
1 Corinthians 9:25 (NIV)

I enjoy participating in road races, triathlons and other athletic competitions. One of my favourite motivational quotes says, 'Finishing "dead last" trumps "did not finish", which trumps "did not start".' Those words remind me to focus on the journey and not the end result. For some, placing in the top of their age division is important, while others just want to start a healthy lifestyle. No matter the goal, the participant must train for the race, which requires discipline, commitment and getting to the starting line!

Paul's letter to the Corinthians compares our spiritual journey to an earthly race. Unlike an earthly race, as Christians we are seeking a reward that will last. Paul tells us that we need strict training in our spiritual lives that takes work, preparation and discipline. Putting in the work requires having a plan and a starting point. Whether our starting point is reading the Bible every day, spending time in prayer with God, devoting ourselves to loving service to others – beginning a life of active faith gives us the opportunity to finish our spiritual journey well.

Prayer: *Dear Lord, give us the strength and courage to begin and continue our spiritual work today. Amen.*

Thought for the day: If I never start, I will never finish.

Steve Wakefield (Alabama, USA)

A simple gift

Read John 15:9–17

Jesus said, 'My command is this: love each other as I have loved you.'
John 15:12 (NIV)

One afternoon I was walking through a park when I saw a woman sitting on a bench. Her hair was in disarray, her face bore a sad expression and her eyes were downcast. In the centre of the park stood an hibiscus tree overflowing with large red flowers. Some of the flowers had fallen on the pavement, so I decided to gather a few and give them to the woman. I saw an immediate change in her demeanour. She said to me: 'Thank you, kind lady, it has been quite a while since someone gave me flowers.' She got up from the bench with a smile on her face as she smelled the flowers and walked away.

After this experience, I could not help but think of the powerful message in John 15:12. Jesus was the greatest example of love, and he invites us to love one another in words and actions. Simple gestures like a gift of flowers, a kind word, a helping hand or breaking bread with someone can brighten others' spirits. May we never hesitate to be messengers of God's powerful love.

Prayer: *Thank you, God, for your extraordinary love for us. Inspire us to love our neighbours as you have loved us. In the name of Jesus. Amen.*

Thought for the day: My words and actions can show God's love to those around me.

Lillian Saldaña (Havana, Cuba)

Searching for my Saviour

Read Matthew 28:16–20

Jesus said, 'Look, I myself will be with you every day until the end of this present age.'
Matthew 28:20 (CEB)

At times in my life I have been hurting from the troubles and pain surrounding me – an argument in the family, mental problems, sickness, anger, blame or doubt. At those times, I have searched frantically for God, worrying that I have lost my connection to my Saviour. The more I focus on my issues, the more distant God's love for me seems. Sometimes I even feel like God is simply apathetic about my distress.

But then I recall finding a lost pair of glasses on top of my head or my lost item in my lap and feeling so silly. I didn't need to become frantic because what I thought was lost was right there with me. It is the same with my Saviour; I have not lost him. I take a breath and once again focus on God.

In his last words to his followers, Jesus told them that he would be with them, and he remains with us today. Through the Holy Spirit, our Saviour will be with us until the end. Though I may not feel a physical presence with me, the Holy Spirit comforts my aching heart, letting me know I have nothing to fear. So now, when I find myself tempted to doubt Jesus' presence with me, I remember that he resides in my heart.

Prayer: *Thank you, Abba Father, for being with us at all times. We pray in the name of Christ and by the power of the Holy Spirit. Amen.*

Thought for the day: My connection to God can never be broken.

Jenny Calvert (Texas, USA)

In God's hands

Read Philippians 4:10–13

God will meet all your needs according to the riches of his glory in Christ Jesus.
Philippians 4:19 (NIV)

The weather has recently changed from warm sunny days to grey chilly days and even colder nights. The leaves have fallen from the trees. With the falling temperatures and frost at night, it is likely that warm-weather creatures will struggle.

Usually, I am removing the dead flowers from my garden at this time of year. So I was surprised when I began my fall garden work and saw that the cosmos flowers with their bright orange and yellow blooms were still going strong. It was wonderful to see the bees and butterflies receiving a much-needed meal. Even as the seasons changed, the needs of these small creatures were still being met.

I remembered the times when I was out of work and could not see a way to pay my bills or feed my family. But God always provided for our needs. As a Christian, I have learned to seek God's help through prayer whenever I'm in need. I rely on Jesus' promise in Matthew 7:7–8: 'Ask and it will be given to you; seek and you will find; knock and the door will be opened to you. For everyone who asks receives; the one who seeks finds; and to the one who knocks, the door will be opened.'

Prayer: *Thank you, creator God, for your love, kindness and grace. Our lives are in your hands, and we depend on you. Amen.*

Thought for the day: God knows what we need and will not leave us wanting.

Charles Small (South Carolina, USA)

From tears to joy

Read Psalm 126:1–6

May those who sow in tears reap with shouts of joy.
Psalm 126:5 (NRSV)

I was sick, and it was getting me down. I wanted to pray for help, but I barely had the energy to sit up or even string a sentence together. When I tried to pray, my words came out in a confused muddle. I felt so disconnected from God, just when I needed God the most.

Worse than my physical illness was the feeling that God wasn't with me. I knew this wasn't the case; God is always with us. God knows our thoughts and hears all our prayers – even the garbled ones. But in this moment I just couldn't feel it.

I told God how awful I felt, how I couldn't feel God's presence, how I was so tired of being unwell and unproductive. I began to say whatever was on my mind in a stream-of-consciousness style. Then I started to cry. That's when I began to feel God's presence again. I talked a bit more, cried some more and I felt God's presence a little more. My hurt and pain had been blocking me from feeling God's presence. Each time I honestly prayed about whatever was on my mind, I felt a little bit closer to God.

Praying isn't always easy. Words don't always roll off the tongue. But with perseverance we can find ways to talk to God and restore our connection, just when we need it the most.

Prayer: *Dear heavenly Father, thank you for always being with us. Help us to feel the joy of your presence. Amen.*

Thought for the day: Sharing my honest thoughts with God can lead to peace.

Kate Orson (Tuscany, Italy)

Rowing or drifting?

Read Hebrews 2:1–4

We must pay the most careful attention, therefore, to what we have heard, so that we do not drift away.
Hebrews 2:1 (NIV)

It was a warm spring day – perfect for fishing. I felt such peace as my husband and I drifted along the calm lake in our inflatable boat. The sun warmed my face, and the gentle breeze pushed us along. We were so focused on our fishing poles that we didn't realise how far we had drifted. What I thought was a gentle breeze was much stronger than I realised. We were heading into the reeds!

We quickly began rowing to avoid getting stuck, but each time our aching arms forced us to stop rowing, the wind took over again and moved our boat. Wet, tired and frustrated, we ended up in a place we didn't want to go.

When I reflected on this later, it occurred to me that my relationship with God is like that experience on the lake. It requires focus to grow in my faith. If I'm not actively rowing towards Jesus, I can easily drift away.

It's easy to get caught up in the winds of the world and end up going in a direction we don't want to go. Our relationship with God, time spent in scripture and our connection to the church body make the difference between moving towards God or drifting away.

Prayer: *Dear God, help us to keep our attention on you and not on the things of this world that cause us to drift away from you. Amen.*

Thought for the day: Are my actions bringing me closer to God?

Denise E. Arzoian (Oregon, USA)

Staying available

Read Romans 12:1–8

In all your ways submit to [the Lord], and he will make your paths straight.
Proverbs 3:6 (NIV)

My ministry entails editing a newsletter to help inmates like me who are on death row. Recently, while I was organising the next issue, an elderly inmate came to my cell and asked me to help him find his glasses. Though a little frustrated at the interruption, I went to help. An hour later, I had just sat back down when another person came to vent to me about his marital problems. I listened. After that, someone else called for me, also needing my time and energy.

I was getting irritated because I felt I couldn't focus on editing the newsletter – the work God had called me to do. I prayed for peace, and God brought a verse to mind: 'In their hearts humans plan their course, but the Lord establishes their steps' (Proverbs 16:9). I realised that although my writing ministry is valuable, sometimes God wants me to serve in unpredictable ways.

It is easy for us to get locked into patterns of service and make ourselves unavailable to God. But we are not our own; we are God's. There are many ways to minister, and God is always at work (see 1 Corinthians 12:4–6). Our job is simply to maintain humble, willing and obedient hearts that follow where God leads.

Prayer: *Loving Father, grant us the wisdom to see your guiding hand and remind us to stay open to unexpected opportunities to serve. Amen.*

Thought for the day: Interruptions can lead me exactly where God wants me.

George T. Wilkerson (Maryland, USA)

Our advocate

Read Psalm 34:17–22

The Spirit helps us in our weakness, for we do not know how to pray as we ought, but that very Spirit intercedes with groanings too deep for words.
Romans 8:26 (NRSV)

When I was a child, my home environment was filled with violence. I felt completely insignificant. When I was only seven or eight years old, I was depressed and harboured dark thoughts bordering on suicide.

As I grew into a teenager, my childhood continued to haunt me, and I experienced lingering thoughts that I did not deserve to live. Then I learned about Jesus, a man who experienced great suffering at the hands of his peers and was crucified. I marvelled at the great injustice he had suffered. I prayed earnestly, asking Jesus to take away my problems. But Jesus Christ taught me instead to forgive my aggressors. Eventually, I came to understand that they treated me the way they did because they could not give me what they did not have.

Even though my parents abandoned me, the Lord welcomed me lovingly with open arms. I learned that I cannot change people, but the Holy Spirit can. My advocate, the Holy Spirit, awakened in me the desire to commit to a new future and the belief that I could choose a new life in Christ. Thanks be to God!

Prayer: *Even before we cry out to you, great God of mercy, you already know our needs. Help us to accept ourselves as beloved children created in your image. Amen.*

Thought for the day: 'The Lord… saves the crushed in spirit' (Psalm 34:18).

María Isabel Rodríguez Carrillo (Pinar del Río, Cuba)

PRAYER FOCUS: YOUNG PEOPLE IN CRISIS

Repurposing our lives

Read Isaiah 41:8–17

'I took you from the ends of the earth, from its farthest corners I called you. I said, "You are my servant"; I have chosen you and have not rejected you.'
Isaiah 41:9 (NIV)

I enjoy turning recycled junk into art. I take items that are going to be discarded – vintage tools, hardware, old china, tiles, game pieces, aluminium cans and other everyday objects – and I generate fresh, unique artwork that conveys a positive message. To redeem a once-valuable item that would have been thrown away gives me great satisfaction!

For a while, especially during the height of the pandemic, I felt insignificant, isolated and purposeless. But then opportunities arose for service projects that could be done at home. I could glorify God and serve others by creatively rejuvenating old ways of serving. Even the little things we do can make an impact when we allow a loving heart and a spirit of service to guide us.

We may feel that we don't have much to offer because we are broken, flawed or lack confidence. But we can be recreated to glorify God, and our brokenness can be renewed. 'We are God's handiwork, created in Christ Jesus to do good works, which God prepared in advance for us to do' (Ephesians 2:10). Regardless of our age or abilities, when we seek opportunities to do good works, our lives can be repurposed to love and serve God.

Prayer: *Lord God, guide us to follow your purpose for our lives each day. Help us to look and listen for ways to serve you. Amen.*

Thought for the day: Even when I feel broken or unworthy, God loves me.

Deb Greenawalt (Pennsylvania, USA)

Never a bother

Read Matthew 6:5–15

Whenever you pray, go into your room and shut the door and pray to your Father who is in secret, and your Father who sees in secret will reward you.
Matthew 6:6 (NRSV)

We get calls from both our sons, but the younger one calls more frequently. He calls not only on birthdays and holidays, but every day. When I was still on staff at the church, he would call so often that when my phone rang during a meeting, our lead pastor would quip, 'Tell Ben I said hello!'

Though Ben's timing was sometimes inconvenient, I never tired of answering. It didn't matter to me that those calls were usually about insignificant things because I just enjoyed talking with him.

Sometimes when I read today's quoted verse, I have wondered why God would be interested in my prayers. After all, God already knows what I need. Then I remember Ben's phone calls.

We need not worry whether our prayers seem important. We are not bothering God when we talk about our concerns. Sure, God knows what we need before we ask, but Jesus teaches us about 'whenever we pray', not 'if we pray'. Why not reach out to God right now? God loves to hear from us!

Prayer: *Loving God, forgive us for doubting your care for us. Remind us that we can always connect with you through prayer. Amen.*

Thought for the day: God never tires of hearing from me.

Peter Caligiuri (Florida, USA)

PRAYER FOCUS: SOMEONE CONCERNED ABOUT BOTHERING GOD   93

Peace in stillness

Read Psalm 46:1–11

In peace I will lie down and sleep, for you alone, Lord, make me dwell in safety.
Psalm 4:8 (NIV)

Last year I was in the hospital for surgery to have my gallbladder removed. It was my first time under general anaesthesia; but lying obediently on the gurney, I breathed myself to sleep. Only after I woke up with a sore and bandaged abdomen did it occur to me what a gesture of trust I had made towards the doctors and technicians. I had put myself completely at their mercy. I had had complete confidence in their integrity and skill.

Why, then, when I was so ready to put myself in the hands of fallible human beings, am I so reluctant to trust in God's integrity and care, to believe in God's promises?

I think of this experience whenever I sit down to pray, attempting to surrender myself to God's will. When my anxieties and petty concerns keep crowding in, preventing me from fully entering into quiet prayer, I try to let go, breathe and feel myself held in a space of love. God provides me with care greater than any human physician. When I surrender to God, God calms my restlessness so that I can experience resurrection life.

Prayer: *Dear Lord, you are with us always. Help us find stillness in our restless souls, so that we can know you and receive your healing power. Amen.*

Thought for the day: I can always trust in the presence of God.

Lory Widmer Hess (Bern, Switzerland)

Making an impression

Read Colossians 3:1–17

As God's choice, holy and loved, put on compassion, kindness, humility, gentleness, and patience.
Colossians 3:12 (CEB)

Sometimes after I put together an outfit that I think looks good, and more importantly is comfortable, my wife will look at me with a smile and ask, 'Why are you leaving the house dressed like that?' So, I change my clothes. We laugh about it, but my wife's attentiveness to the clothes I wear reminds me that how we present ourselves makes an impression on others.

With Christ, we are given the grace to clothe ourselves with love, kindness, compassion and patience.

Early Christianity grew in part because outsiders witnessed the changed lives, good qualities and virtues of those who followed Christ. As Jesus said in John 13:35, 'This is how everyone will know that you are my disciples, when you love each other.' Jesus taught his disciples to show the world what they believe and where they find hope.

I still find it tempting to go back to old patterns of living. But I am constantly reminded of Jesus' transforming grace, which allows the world to see Christ through us.

Prayer: *Holy God, guide us to clothe ourselves in love and kindness. May the world see Christ when they look at us. Amen.*

Thought for the day: How well do my actions and attitudes reflect my faith?

Ryan Stratton (Texas, USA)

Comfort in grief

Read Psalm 139:13–18

Your eyes saw my unformed body; all the days ordained for me were written in your book before one of them came to be.
Psalm 139:16 (NIV)

I received news that no one ever wants to hear. My three-month prenatal ultrasound showed no signs of a heartbeat. I would never hold my precious baby in my arms. The sadness was overwhelming.

After the initial waves of sadness, I felt a sense of shame for my intense sorrow. My mind told me that I shouldn't feel such anguish over an early pregnancy loss and that this amount of grief should be reserved for late miscarriages or for people who have lost loved ones after years together. I wanted to keep my grief a secret so that no one would think I was overreacting.

But these feelings of shame and embarrassment were quickly replaced with something God had written on my heart years ago. Psalm 139 reminded me that this child was lovingly created by God and that God treasured all of my baby's days.

Remembering that God knows and values my baby has comforted me in my grief, and it has helped me to be open to God's grace that transforms our pain.

Prayer: *Father God, thank you for comforting us when we mourn. Thank you for the gift of your word that offers peace during difficult times. Help us to be open to your transforming grace. Amen.*

Thought for the day: God loves me all the days of my life.

Angela Sisco (Alberta, Canada)

Loving guidance

Read Luke 19:1–10
The Son of Man came to seek out and to save the lost.
Luke 19:10 (NRSV)

Once when I was young, I spotted a ripe mango high in our tree and climbed to get it – a common practice in my village. But when I was high up, the branch I was standing on broke. I grabbed a branch above my head but was unable to get a foothold. Seeing me hanging there, a group of men rushed over and encouraged me to let go, promising to catch me. But I couldn't let go. Then my brother climbed the tree and reached out to me, calmly telling me to stretch my leg towards him. He supported my leg as I moved closer, and then he placed my foot on the stump of the broken branch. With his support and encouragement, I climbed down safely.

In today's scripture story, Zacchaeus was not physically in danger, but he was lost – socially and spiritually isolated and far from God. He needed a saviour to guide him back to God. When Jesus saw Zacchaeus in the sycamore tree, he reached out to him and showed him a new way to live.

We all need a loving and supportive guide to help us. How encouraging it is to know that Jesus finds us wherever we are and offers loving support, gently empowering and guiding us.

Prayer: *Loving God, thank you for calling us to you through your Son, Jesus Christ. Open our hearts to receive your support and guidance at all times. In Jesus' name. Amen.*

Thought for the day: No matter where I am, Jesus is reaching out to me.

Owar Ojha Ojulu (Pennsylvania, USA)

PRAYER FOCUS: THOSE WHO FEEL ISOLATED

Shared blessings

Read Psalm 8:1–9

Every good gift, every perfect gift, comes from above. These gifts come down from the Father, the creator of the heavenly lights, in whose character there is no change at all.
James 1:17 (CEB)

My 25-year-old grandson is in prison on charges of breaking and entering. He calls me each week around 6.30 pm. On a recent summer afternoon, he called two hours early, and I feared something was wrong. In a worried voice, I asked whether he was okay.

He replied that he was fine but simply couldn't wait to tell me about a good thing that happened to him that day. Through the narrow window on one wall, he had seen a flock of brightly coloured goldfinches flitting around a maple tree.

I imagined the smile on his face as he said, 'Gran, I wish you could have seen them.' I recalled the many times I had shared God's natural blessings with him as he grew up. Speckled fawns, hard-shelled turtles, yellow swallowtail butterflies, showy blue dragonflies and many yellow finches frequented my backyard and had delighted all my grandchildren.

My grandson had received a blessing that day, and he passed the blessing on to me. No matter what our state in life, God knows our need for blessings. My grandson's call taught me that God does not forget those who are in prison. God sends blessings to them and also uses them to bring bits of joy to others.

Prayer: *Creator God, thank you for the countless blessings you bestow on us. Help us pass these blessings on to others. Amen.*

Thought for the day: What blessing will I share with someone today?

Jewel Deane Suddath (North Carolina, USA)

Working for good

Read Philippians 2:12–18
We know that in all things God works for the good of those who love him, who have been called according to his purpose.
Romans 8:28 (NIV)

When I attended the memorial service of a person very dear to me, a reference was made to Romans 8:28. It troubled me to say 'all things work together for the good' about a dear friend's death. But the words remained with me, and I revisited the text, trying to make sense of it. I decided to start keeping a journal where I noted different situations – good and bad – to see what the outcome was.

One particular experience helped me to appreciate fully how God worked for good in my life. I joined an organisation where, despite my being a senior manager, responsibilities were taken away from me without consultation. To fill the emptiness, I started to coach young colleagues informally. My manager noticed and acknowledged that I was good at helping people develop their skills and talents. I was encouraged to seek appropriate training, and the organisation would pay for it. What a blessing! God had truly worked out all things for my good.

Over time, as I continued with my journal, I was amazed to see the ways that indeed God was working for good, even when the circumstances seemed otherwise.

Prayer: *Heavenly Father, thank you for showering us with blessings in all life's circumstances. In Jesus' name. Amen.*

Thought for the day: A challenging situation can be a gift from God.

Makgoshi Sindane (South Africa)

A winter garden

Read Psalm 27:7–14

I have sure faith that I will experience the Lord's goodness in the land of the living!

Psalm 27:13 (CEB)

For some reason I decided to visit one of my favourite gardens in the middle of January. The trees had no leaves, the daylilies were trimmed to the ground and the herb garden was a drab brown. I walked to the corner where one of my favourites – the white ginger lily – usually bloomed, but it had also been trimmed back. The whole garden was grey and brown.

But as I turned to leave, a tiny flash of yellow caught my eye. A small yellow crocus was peeking through the sod – a speck of colour in a sea of brown. I was filled with a sense of hope. Spring was coming.

The past few years had been a kind of winter for me, with the pandemic, personal sickness, the loss of two friends and the death of my younger sister. It was a time of many losses, one after another. Now God spoke to me through the little crocus: spring will arrive again. Hope was, and still is, alive.

Prayer: *Dear Lord, thank you for your power at work in the world. Help us to know that hope is alive and to notice the ways you are speaking to us. Amen.*

Thought for the day: God speaks to me through nature.

Mike Bertoglio (Georgia, USA)

What do we need?

Read John 1:1–5

[The Lord] has shown you… what is good. And what does the Lord require of you? To act justly and to love mercy and to walk humbly with your God.
Micah 6:8 (NIV)

This past Christmas at church we decided to do something different. During the first week of Advent the sanctuary was set up as normal: wreaths and candles in the windows, a decorated tree up front, a full crèche scene, and candles for each Sunday of Advent with the words 'peace', 'love', 'joy' and 'hope' in front of them. Every week that followed, though, something was removed. First the wreaths came down from the windows. Then the tree. Eventually, by Christmas Eve, only Mary and Joseph were left.

During the service, the children were called up to the simple scene that remained. But before they placed Jesus in the manger, they were asked why we took down all the decorations except Mary and Joseph. A young boy responded, 'Because we don't need them.' He was asked, 'What do we need, then?'

His answer put tears in our eyes. 'Peace, love…' And the congregation helped him finish, 'joy and hope'. With that, baby Jesus – who is the source of peace, love, joy and hope – was placed in the manger. Christmas is not the bows or the presents, the cards or the decorations; it is the celebration of the birth of our Saviour, God incarnate. And for that, all we need is an open heart.

Prayer: *Holy One, help us to remember the simplicity into which you came. Remind us that the only necessary preparations for this day are for our hearts to be open to receive you. Amen.*

Thought for the day: Christmas is peace, love, joy and hope.

Dawn M. Adams (Massachusetts, USA)

PRAYER FOCUS: THOSE OVERWHELMED BY HOLIDAY PREPARATIONS

Healed and set free

Read Luke 13:10–17

Heal me, Lord, and I will be healed; save me and I will be saved, for you are the one I praise.
Jeremiah 17:14 (NIV)

For several years I suffered with severe back pain, and I used a metal belt for support. I prayed that God would heal me, but I could not stop using the belt. Then one day, I took off the belt and discovered that the pain had disappeared and I was able to walk freely again. Now I know that God had been healing me all those years; I just had to let go of the belt to discover God's miraculous healing touch.

My experience reminded me of the account of the woman healed by Jesus in Luke 13. She had been unable to stand up straight for 18 years. Jesus called to her saying, 'Woman, you are set free from your infirmity.' He then put his hands on her, and she was healed. So she straightened up and praised God.

We might struggle to open ourselves up to accept God's grace. We often cling to thoughts, beliefs and actions that hold us back. But when we let them go, we allow God to work on us and set us free.

Prayer: *Heavenly Father, you are our healer and sustainer. Help us to receive your grace and healing so that we may bless others. Amen.*

Thought for the day: I will open myself to God's healing.

Navamani Peter (Karnataka, India)

Not always easy

Read Philippians 3:7–14

I press on towards the goal to win the prize for which God has called me heavenward in Christ Jesus.
Philippians 3:14 (NIV)

During my younger years in India, I attended a Christian retreat in the Himalayan Mountains. After the retreat was over, my friend and I decided to climb Naina Peak in Nainital, farther north.

We started climbing early in the morning. It was a hard, steep climb. After an hour or so, I was close to giving up. But a voice kept urging me, 'Do not give up.' So I kept climbing slowly. Finally, we reached the peak. The sight of the Himalayan Mountains covered with snow was breathtaking and beautiful.

As I read Philippians 3:14, I think about the ways following Christ resembles that hike. Following Christ is not easy. Truly following Christ requires full commitment and wholehearted faithfulness. And thankfully, our trials refine and empower us to keep growing earnestly in Christ's discipleship.

Prayer: *Dear Lord, even when the journey is challenging, give us the strength to keep following you faithfully. Amen.*

Thought for the day: Focusing on Christ helps me to grow in my faith.

Baldeo Singh (Nebraska, USA)

No greater love

Read 1 John 3:16–24

Greater love has no one than this: to lay down one's life for one's friends.
John 15:13 (NIV)

Sometimes we have difficulty understanding the great love our Saviour has for each one of us. Jesus will likely not ask us to die for our friends, yet he does ask us to love one another as he loved us.

I experienced that kind of love in my life when I had a serious health problem that prevented me from taking care of myself upon discharge from the hospital. Expecting I would need help for only a few months, my aunt moved in with me. But over a year later, I still need her help.

As I meditated on the scripture above, I realised that my aunt has truly shown her love by laying down her life for me. By moving in with me to care for me, she has left behind her home of over 50 years, her friends, her favourite restaurants, her doctors, her bank, her familiar stores and her neighbours. She has continued to care for me even as she deals with her own cancer diagnosis and treatment. She has sacrificed much. My aunt is living out the scripture, 'Greater love has no one than this: to lay down one's life for one's friends.'

Prayer: *Loving God, help us to be sensitive to the needs of those around us so that we can show your sacrificial love to others. Remind us to show gratitude to those who love us. In Jesus' holy name. Amen.*

Thought for the day: How will I show sacrificial love to someone today?

Debbi Whitezell (Pennsylvania, USA)

God will provide

Read Matthew 6:25–34

Look at the birds of the air; they do not sow or reap or store away in barns, and yet your heavenly Father feeds them. Are you not much more valuable than they?
Matthew 6:26 (NIV)

With joy I watch for the local newspaper announcement: 'She's here!' Every year I look forward to news about Grandma Mount Yamamoto, the female Steller's sea eagle that roosts on Mount Yamamoto during the winter. Since 1998, she has flown in and made the mountain her winter home.

One of the oldest eagles in Japan, Grandma Mount Yamamoto is considered a national treasure. Despite her age, she still glides gracefully on her beautiful outspread wings and catches fish with expert skill. In February, she takes off for the breeding grounds in Russia's Kamchatka Peninsula.

This great eagle's annual migration and faithful return each winter is an inspiration to me. I think it is noble to single-mindedly follow the path God has given us and trust that God will take care of the rest. Scripture reminds me that God cares for the birds of the air, and in the same way will provide for my needs. I feel God's protection when I entrust everything to God.

Prayer: *Father God, thank you for your loving care. Help us to entrust everything to you and single-mindedly serve you. Amen.*

Thought for the day: I feel protected and at peace because God is with me.

Chieko Tamura (Shiga Prefecture, Japan)

PRAYER FOCUS: WILDLIFE CONSERVATION EFFORTS

Sleepless nights

Read Psalm 149:1–9

Let the faithful exult in glory; let them sing for joy on their couches.
Psalm 149:5 (NRSV)

Neither my wife nor I sleep well these days. While she usually remains in bed on restless nights, I go to the other room and sit on the couch with a book or a game of solitaire until sleep overtakes me. Those nights are full of frustration and anxiety. I have to avoid looking at a clock so I don't count the hours until my alarm goes off. My thoughts are filled with worries from the previous day and the one ahead.

Psalm 149 doesn't seem like an obvious source of comfort. It is filled with commands that seem directed at the listener – imperatives to praise and be joyful. For the longest time this made me feel worse. Singing for joy is the most distant thing from my mind during my sleepless hours.

But I've begun to wonder if this exhortation could perhaps be directed to the Holy One. Let these faithful ones rejoice and be joyful can also be a prayer, a request, a plea to the Divine for those who are struggling to rejoice. Perhaps it could even be a prayer for those of us who, in the wee hours of the morning, feel anything but joy.

Prayer: *Dear Jesus, be with us when our minds are filled with worries. With the grace of your joy, comfort those who lie awake in the night. Amen.*

Thought for the day: God is with me even when I'm not feeling joyful.

Jonathan Bennett (Tennessee, USA)

PRAYER FOCUS: THOSE EXPERIENCING INSOMNIA

Abundant fruit

Read John 15:1–8

Jesus said, 'I am the vine; you are the branches. If you remain in me and I in you, you will bear much fruit; apart from me you can do nothing.'
John 15:5 (NIV)

On a cool summer morning I eagerly strolled into a blueberry patch with my empty bucket. Rows of blueberry bushes lined the country landscape as birds sang sweetly in the distance. Branches drooped with different shades of blueberries – green unripe ones, red developing ones and bright blue ripe ones. I searched for the ripe blueberries and gingerly placed them in my bucket.

Then a large broken branch with wilting fruit caught my attention. I quickly picked the ripe berries, but I knew that the green berries on the broken branch would not ripen. They would not receive the nutrients they needed.

This broken branch reminded me of the importance of staying connected to God through faith in Jesus. In the same way, we can only produce enduring fruits of the Holy Spirit (see Galatians 5:22–23) by abiding in a personal relationship with Jesus. On our own we cannot do anything of eternal value. Spending time in prayer and Bible study enables us to produce spiritual fruit so that we bless others and glorify God.

Prayer: *Lord Jesus, thank you for producing spiritual fruit in us as we spend time with you. Help us encourage others and bring you glory. Amen.*

Thought for the day: Staying connected to God helps me to flourish.

Heather Hagstrom (Kansas, USA)

The gift of love

Read 1 John 4:7–12

This is love: not that we loved God, but that he loved us and sent his Son as an atoning sacrifice for our sins. Dear friends, since God so loved us, we also ought to love one another.
1 John 4:10–11 (NIV)

As a child, I always looked forward to Christmas because we usually travelled back home to visit our extended family. We gave and received lots of gifts and ate nice meals together. I remember my mum and aunties cooking large meals together – spending almost all day in the kitchen. Those meals were served to us in large dishes and trays while we all sat together on the floor and enjoyed them. We also shared gifts and food with villagers in need. Spending Christmas together like this created a special bond. The love we had for each other was easy to see, and it has stayed with me throughout my life.

My Christmas experience as a child reminds me of what God expects of us, which is to share God's love for us through our love for others. The season of Christmas is a great opportunity to spread the love of God to family, friends and everyone around us by spending quality time with them, sharing gifts and meals, and even sharing the word of God together. Through these actions, we can radiate the love of God, teach others how to love and create long-lasting memories with the people around us.

Prayer: *Dear Lord, give us the grace to follow your example. Help us to love those around us. In Jesus' name. Amen.*

Thought for the day: Because God loves me, I will love others.

Chioma Fatubaro (Lagos, Nigeria)

A song in the storm

Read Lamentations 3:22–25

Sing to God, sing in praise of his name, extol him who rides on the clouds; rejoice before him – his name is the Lord.
Psalm 68:4 (NIV)

Watching the flashing light fill my bedroom, I listened to the thunder and rain outside my window. Despite the darkness of the storm, dawn was breaking. I could hear birds singing, and my heart was filled with joy. The birds did not allow the stormy conditions to silence their morning song.

The sound of the birds reminded me that behind the clouds the sun was still rising, ushering in a new day. My feathered friends bolstered my faith. No matter what blows through my life, I should never let the conditions stop my praise. No storm could ever stop the sunlight from breaking the darkness of night.

It can be easy to forget the light of God. Frequently I hear people ask, 'Where is God in all of this?' When that question rises up in my heart, I quickly remind myself, God is with us – Immanuel. God is our healer. God is our peace. Great is God's faithfulness. Storms will always be part of life, but like the birds we can weather the storms by keeping songs of praise on our lips.

Prayer: *Ever-present God, you are our shelter during the storms of life. Rescue us from darkness, and bring us into your marvellous light. Amen.*

Thought for the day: Even through the storms, I will praise God.

Winter J. Rose (Maryland, USA)

PRAYER FOCUS: GRATITUDE FOR GOD'S PRESENCE

A living example

Read Matthew 25:31–46

The King will reply, 'Truly I tell you, whatever you did for one of the least of these brothers and sisters of mine, you did for me.'
Matthew 25:40 (NIV)

My cellmate for the past eight months has been a 55-year-old man named Russ who suffers from moderate dementia. Having completed his sentence, Russ was released from prison last week with absolutely no support from anyone in the outside world. His future seems bleak.

During the time we shared our tiny prison cell, I cared for him as if he were my brother. It was not easy. I had to tell him when to eat, to walk him through his daily routine and to share what little I have with him. But I also had the privilege of sharing my faith and being an example of how Christ calls us to live in Matthew 25.

Through this man who has been neglected by society, I learned so much about what it means to live as a Christian in humility, patience and love – virtues that are hard to live by in this environment. As Russ left our cell for the last time, he thanked me for all I had done for him. But I know that I was richly blessed to be chosen by God to live out Christ's love to someone who is 'one of the least of these'.

Prayer: *Heavenly Father, continue to give us opportunities to treat others as we would treat you. Amen.*

Thought for the day: I will treat everyone with the same kindness and love I would show to Christ.

Christopher M. King (Virginia, USA)

Celebrate the moment

Read Psalm 104:24–35

Teach us to number our days, that we may gain a heart of wisdom.
Psalm 90:12 (NIV)

One Saturday evening, my family and I had just had a good dinner. On our walk home, we decided to stop by the grocery store for a few things. It was a clear night. My son and I waited for my husband outside the store. 'Look, Mum,' my son said, pointing to the moon. It was a beautiful view of the full moon gleaming in the night sky. I immediately took out my phone and started taking photo after photo, but my son encouraged me to put away my phone and appreciate the moment with him instead. As we gazed at the amazingly beautiful moon, I gave my son a tight hug.

That evening with my son taught me to be grateful and appreciate all that God is doing in our lives. It is important to value the ordinary moments and days God has given us. Psalm 90:12 says, 'Teach us to number our days, that we may gain a heart of wisdom.' We cannot know what tomorrow will bring. Therefore, let's dedicate today and every day to God – one day at a time.

Prayer: *Dear God, fill our hearts with gratitude so that we will appreciate all you do for us each day. Amen.*

Thought for the day: I will be present in the moment God is giving me.

Lei Garcia-Bote (Kuala Lumpur, Malaysia)

Room for the manger

Read 1 Timothy 6:6–12

Desire [God's] kingdom and these things will be given to you as well.
Luke 12:31 (CEB)

Due to limited space, disorganisation and too much stuff that I fail to discard, my home is not tidy. Especially as the holidays approach, it seems that I add to the clutter daily: new things to read, recipes to try, novel gadgets, unique seasonal foods. There are no empty spaces, no cleared areas waiting for commemorative displays. As Advent arrives each year, I wonder where I will put the two small manger scenes.

Somehow, it happens. In the bedroom I put away the empty clothes hangers, hang up coats and fold blankets, and a spot opens up. In the living room I discard some old catalogues and colourful advertising brochures, put the sweets dish away in a cupboard and move the radio to a lower shelf, freeing up space on top of a small bookshelf. I delight in the lack of clutter and the sight of the simple manger scenes.

This annual ritual reminds me of what is most important: Jesus. When we set aside some of the details and distractions of our lives, we make room for Jesus. The simple manger scene with Jesus at the centre can lead us to contemplate what is truly important.

Prayer: *Dear God, may our focus always remain on you and your love. Amen.*

Thought for the day: Removing clutter from my life makes more room for Jesus.

April Bogert (New York, USA)

Trusting God

Read Psalm 112:1–10

Out of my distress I called on the Lord; the Lord answered me and set me in a broad place.
Psalm 118:5 (NRSV)

As I write this, my eldest daughter, Heaven, just turned eight. She was diagnosed with generalised absence seizures in April 2022. This was perhaps the most painful news we had ever heard, since it involved the health of our child. I still recall the pain I felt when my daughter softly said, 'I will fight this, Dad.' I cried with my whole family.

Heaven needed to undergo an MRI so her physician could determine what medication and treatment she would need. While waiting for the MRI, we spent many long nights in distress. However, we also gained strength and held on to our faith. We entrusted everything to God.

After Heaven underwent the MRI, her physician told us that her brain was functioning normally, and medication was all that was needed. Her physician was amazed. I told the physician that many people had been praying, and we were very thankful.

After six months of taking medication, Heaven is almost fully recovered, and she has not had another seizure. Truly, God is faithful. When we trust in God, God is with us.

Prayer: *Gracious God, be with those who live with chronic conditions. May all those in distress find solace in your loving arms. Amen.*

Thought for the day: Even during troubling situations, I will hold on to my faith.

Hector S. Sadac (Isabela, Philippines)

The gate

Read John 10:1–10

Jesus said, 'I am the gate; whoever enters through me will be saved. They will come in and go out, and find pasture'.
John 10:9 (NIV)

As a friend and I were talking, she mentioned how her dog often lies in the doorway of any room she is in. I said, 'Our dog Lucy does the same thing. It's so inconvenient to step over her. Why do our dogs do that?' With an animal science degree, my friend had much insight into animal behaviour. She suggested that by lying in the doorway, they knew when we left and when we came back. They were shepherding us.

I remembered a lesson that we taught the youth at church about one of the 'I am' statements of Jesus – 'I am the gate'. In the lesson, we talked about how the shepherd would lie across the open gap in the sheep pen and literally become the gate to the pen. He did this to keep the sheep from straying or to prevent an intruder from harming the sheep. Jesus was saying that he is our shepherd and that he is watching over us.

Now, when I see Lucy in the doorway, I don't see it as an inconvenience. I see it as a reminder of Christ's loving care for us all and remember that Jesus is our good shepherd.

Prayer: *Dear God, thank you for your never-ending care for us through Jesus Christ. In his name we pray. Amen.*

Thought for the day: Jesus is the gateway to abundant life.

Beverly Varnado (Georgia, USA)

The joy of Christmas

Read Isaiah 9:1–7

The shepherds returned, glorifying and praising God for all the things they had heard and seen, which were just as they had been told.
Luke 2:20 (NIV)

In my country, Christmas decorations are not common on city streets. They are usually only present in shopping centres or hotels. But there is one location downtown that puts up decorations every year, and before Christmas, I always visit this place to feel the joy of the season.

This year, however, I was sad to discover that there were no decorations in that place. I even visited again on Christmas Eve to check, but the area was still empty. It felt like this Christmas would be less joyous.

However, when I got home, I realised that my joy should not depend on outward displays, such as lights and ornaments. The joy of Christmas should come from within my heart, preparing to welcome the birth of Jesus, the Prince of Peace. Of course it would be fun if Christmas were celebrated extravagantly where I live, but even if I celebrate in a simple way without festive decorations and parties, the joy of Christmas can still fill my heart.

Prayer: *O glorious God, we rejoice over the birth of Christ, the Prince of Peace. Fill our hearts with the joy of Christmas today. Amen.*

Thought for the day: I can joyfully celebrate Christmas, even without decorations and festivities.

Juita Kartini (Jakarta, Indonesia)

A persistent sparrow

Read Psalm 31:19–24

Be strong and take heart, all you who hope in the Lord.
Psalm 31:24 (NIV)

Once, not far from my home, I saw a large flock of sparrows landing on a telephone wire. The line was packed with birds sitting nearly shoulder to shoulder. One bird, late to arrive, could not find a place to perch. With great persistence, it kept fluttering back and forth looking for a spot to sit. The bird finally found a place barely wide enough to accommodate it. That tiny bird did not give up.

This observation made me think about hope. Hope in God is expressed eloquently in Psalm 31. Such hope is rare in our world today, where we so often see violence and division among people. When our society seems to offer us little reason to feel optimistic, are we not more likely to find hope in our faith and its timeless values?

Sometimes, when I struggle with difficulties of my own, I might become discouraged and feel overwhelmed. Nevertheless, I can take heart in remembering the persistence of the tiny sparrow and the words of Psalm 31. With God's help and guidance, I can keep persevering with hope.

Prayer: *Dear Lord, may we remember to follow your guidance. May we not be afraid to be hopeful. Amen.*

Thought for the day: I will persevere in my faith.

William Balch (Pennsylvania, USA)

Burdens into joy

Read Genesis 18:9–14

Is anything too hard for the Lord? I will return to you at the appointed time next year, and Sarah will have a son.
Genesis 18:14 (NIV)

I am at a point in my life where nothing seems to be working out. I am a first-year university student with too many bills to pay, parents who are on the verge of separating and lots of anxiety about the future. I do not know what lies ahead.

What I do know for sure is that God is a miracle-working God. But there are moments when I find it difficult to see even a tiny glimpse of hope. I find myself wondering, Does God actually care? Can God turn my heart's burdens into joy?

There are so many reasons for my heart to worry, to be anxious, to be restless. But I find peace knowing that nothing is impossible for God. After all, God was able to give Abraham and Sarah a child despite their old age. Remembering this, I find myself rejoicing in all my battles. The story of Abraham and Sarah is a call to trust the Lord even more in situations that we cannot understand. It is in those situations where God's name is glorified. We may not be able to see the solutions for our problems, but we can trust that God can. Nothing is impossible for our great God.

Prayer: *Dear Lord, help us to trust your timing and your plans. You are our source of hope. Amen.*

Thought for the day: No matter what, God is faithful.

Theresa Reves (Rizal, Philippines)

Beautiful lights

Read Matthew 5:13–16

Walk while you have the light, before darkness overtakes you…
Believe in the light while you have the light, so that you may become
children of light.
John 12:35–36 (NIV)

I love the lights at this time of year as I drive through neighbourhood streets, sit in the glow of a Christmas tree and walk through my town's multicoloured display. However, these beautiful light displays require work. At our house, light strands always malfunction. This year we struggled to find a working strand to weave through an unlit section of our garland.

While staring at the dark section of garland, I was reminded that though we may be connected to the same power through our relationship with Christ, we do not all enter the Christmas season with bright spirits. The same decorations that bring me joy and comfort can trigger painful memories for others. I remember Christmases marked by grief: the death of a loved one, a job ending and even the loss of a pregnancy. Having endured those challenging years, I know not everyone experiences the delights of the holidays.

In John 12:36, Jesus urges his disciples to connect with him so they can become children of the light, shining his light in the world. We are called to reach out to those with heavy hearts through hugs, prayers and acts of kindness, weaving God's light through their lives.

Prayer: *Dear Jesus, as we celebrate your birth, may we focus on your love, hope and purpose. Bring your light to those who need comfort and strength. Amen.*

Thought for the day: I will share Christ's light and love with those whose hearts are heavy this season.

Peg Arnold (Colorado, USA)

Not shaken

Read Psalm 3:1–8

I call out to the Lord, and he answers me from his holy mountain.
Psalm 3:4 (NIV)

I was first diagnosed with an anxiety disorder when I was 15. Sometimes anxiety strikes me like lightning, and I feel like I'm gasping for breath. My heart pounds, and I feel like electricity is coursing through my veins. My mind plays the same worries over and over again. What if I'm not good enough? What if people don't like me? What if God is mad at me?

Today I'm in my 30s. Years of psychological treatment have improved my life immensely, but my anxious tendencies have never fully left me and likely never will. While I would never wish these moments of intense, painful worry on anyone, through them I have grown in my relationship with God. My connection to God feels more raw and real when I cry out to God in moments when I am powerless against my thoughts. When my coping mechanisms fail me, my Lord does not.

Psalm 3 inspires me to pour out my worries and lay them at God's feet. God is not shaken by our worries. In the depths of our despair, God is a secure presence we can hold on to. We don't have to pretend that everything is fine. God does not require pretty, upbeat prayers but can bear the weight of our heaviest burdens.

Prayer: *Dear Lord God, thank you for hearing us when we call out to you. Help us to trust in your strength to sustain us through any trial. Amen.*

Thought for the day: At all times I will bring my worries to God.

Jillian Bell (Ontario, Canada)

Healing song

Read 1 Samuel 16:14–23

David would take up his lyre and play. Then relief would come to Saul; he would feel better.
1 Samuel 16:23 (NIV)

God blesses us with gifts that bring us fulfilment and joy and can bring healing to others. Music, singing, dancing and art are used in therapeutic settings to help with mental health issues such as depression. They are also used for degenerative illnesses of the mind, like dementia. Research shows that choral singing brings many physical health benefits and also enhances emotional well-being.

I was struck recently when reading 1 Samuel that the healing power of music was recognised even then. Saul's servants, seeing their king tormented by an evil spirit, suggested that they find someone to play the harp for him, so that the spirit might leave him. Saul ordered them to do so, and David was summoned to attend to him. This was the means by which David first came to meet King Saul. The Bible records that David's playing was soothing and effective.

My own experience of the healing power of music was when my mother had Alzheimer's. We sang together in her care home and were both uplifted. The songs took my mother back to old times and fond memories, and she was happy. Although unable to hold a conversation with me, she could still recall the words to many songs and even learn new songs. To see and hear this made my own heart soar.

Prayer: *Thank you, Father, for all your gifts of creativity. Grant that we may share them with others. Amen.*

Thought for the day: 'Sing and make music from your heart to the Lord' (Ephesians 5:19).

Faith Ford (England, United Kingdom)

Winter solstice

Read Psalm 145:17–21

The Lord is near to all who call on him.
Psalm 145:18 (NIV)

I was reading Psalm 145 on the winter solstice, the day of the year when there is the least amount of daylight. As I read of the Lord's grace, compassion, faithfulness and presence, I was reassured to remember that for the next six months the days will get longer and brighter.

That is a purely physical observation, but I was also reminded that in our spiritual and emotional lives there are likewise winter seasons, times of more darkness than light, times of grief as when a loved one dies. We regret their passing, but at the same time we rejoice that, for those who are Christians, they have moved on to something better. That does not alter the fact that we mourn their passing, and like the daylight hours after the winter solstice, it takes time before we emerge into the springtime.

It has now been five years since my husband died, and I still have days of grief, even though I know he is in heaven and fit and well. But those years have been a time of walking into spring and finding anew the love of God.

Prayer: *Dear Lord, comfort us when we experience the dark night of the soul, and help us to rejoice again in your love. Amen.*

Thought for the day: No day is so dark that God's love cannot penetrate it.

Hilary Hartley (England, United Kingdom)

Shining Christ's light

Read John 8:12–18

Jesus spoke to the people again, saying, 'I am the light of the world. Whoever follows me won't walk in darkness but will have the light of life'.
John 8:12 (CEB)

During the Christmas season, it is customary in my part of Nigeria for people to travel – sometimes from all over the world – to their respective villages. It is a time to visit our roots and spend time with family and friends.

One year I visited a cousin who lives in a rural community. We chatted outside late into the night. Electric lights illuminated the community and made it quite welcoming. Since we were in the tropics, we were surrounded by giant trees. The noises around us were like music to my ears. Bats, owls and biting insects began to emerge. But while we were talking, the lights suddenly went out. The surrounding darkness was intense. I realised then what a difference light makes.

We started talking about the impact of light on a community. Eventually discussion turned to spiritual light and Christmas – how light came into the world through the birth of our Lord Jesus Christ. As we celebrate Christmas, sometimes we gloss over its significance. The light of Christ changed the world; it is our duty as believers to keep it shining!

Prayer: *Dear God, make us light to the world, at Christmastime and all year. May our lives bring glory to you. Amen.*

Thought for the day: I will live in a way that brings Christ's light to the world.

Zeph Dim (Lagos, Nigeria)

God of second chances

Read Isaiah 61:1–3

[The Lord has anointed me] to comfort all who mourn… to bestow on them a crown of beauty instead of ashes.
Isaiah 61:2–3 (NIV)

When I interviewed with Jon for a job at his home-care company, I was struggling. He asked why I had left my previous job, which I had been fired from. I wish I could say that I admitted the truth, but I wasn't quite that brave because I needed this new job. I told Jon that I hadn't been given the resources to do what was expected of me at my previous job, so I felt that I needed to move on. This was true but not the whole truth. Jon hired me.

After working for him for a short time, the subject of my previous job came up again. With my heart pounding, I took a deep breath and decided to tell him the whole truth. Jon smiled and said, 'I thought as much. I could read between the lines. But God is a God of second chances, and we are a company of second chances'.

In the Bible, there are many examples of people who got second chances. Rahab was a prostitute. David was a murderer. Paul persecuted Christians. Yet God worked through each of them. Through Jesus Christ, God offers us all second chances. May we use them to see the beauty in life, experience the joy of living and give praise to God. And may we bless others with forgiveness, compassion and kindness – giving them second chances too.

Prayer: *Dear Father, thank you for showing us compassion. Help us to extend the same compassion and generosity to those around us. Amen.*

Thought for the day: Just as God has done with me, I'll give someone a second chance.

Sue Kerrigan (Washington, USA)

God with us

Read Psalm 139:7–12

Paul wrote, 'I am persuaded, that neither death, nor life, nor angels, nor principalities, nor powers, nor things present, nor things to come, nor height, nor depth, nor any other creature, shall be able to separate us from the love of God, which is in Christ Jesus our Lord'.
Romans 8:38–39 (KJV)

Years ago, I lived in a small town in Honduras while working with a team on a year-long project. As Christmas approached, I felt sad instead of excited. For the first time, I would not spend Christmas with my family. I felt alone.

On Christmas Eve, I heard distant singing. I looked out the window and saw a Las Posadas procession coming up the street. People carrying candles followed a boy and girl who were dressed like Joseph and Mary. The procession stopped at each house and sang a request for shelter, re-enacting the Holy Family's search for a place to stay in Bethlehem. The homeowners would listen, shake their heads and wave the group away. Eventually, they sang at the house across the street from me. The homeowner threw open his door and invited everyone in. I went outside and followed the crowd.

The homeowner had a manger ready in his front room. On Christmas Day, a figure of the Christ-child appeared in the manger. The house was left open for anyone who wanted to pay homage to the baby Jesus. What a joy it was to visit him right next door! This reminded me that no matter where we are, God's door is always open.

Prayer: *Dear Lord, thank you for being with us and for providing reminders of your constant presence and love. Amen.*

Thought for the day: Nothing can separate us from the love of God.

Mary Neumann (Georgia, USA)

A son is given

Read Matthew 1:18–25

An angel of the Lord appeared to [Joseph] in a dream and said, 'Joseph… do not be afraid to take Mary as your wife, for the child conceived in her is from the Holy Spirit. She will bear a son, and you are to name him Jesus, for he will save his people from their sins'.
Matthew 1:20–21 (NRSV)

My son's birth was a gift for my wife, Allyssa, and me. I remember the day he was born and the stress I felt as Allyssa had to have a C-section; I was with her the entire time. When the doctor delivered our son and I heard his first cry, I understood how it must have felt for Joseph to witness the birth of Jesus.

While the birth of any child is a gift, the birth of Jesus Christ was God's greatest gift. When Jesus was born, Mary and Joseph knew he had come to bring salvation to all.

During Christmas we can get so caught up in looking for the perfect gift for others that we miss the perfect gift given to us by God. Salvation through Jesus means that we are eternally loved by God. From this gift of love, we are inspired to love one another. Such a gift is free for all to take, and once accepted, it is life changing.

Prayer: *Dear Lord, thank you for the perfect gift of your Son and for the salvation that came through him. In his name we pray. Amen.*

Thought for the day: Jesus is the most perfect gift ever given.

Steven McNeal (North Carolina, USA)

A global connection

Read Psalm 42:1–11

Why, my soul, are you downcast? Why so disturbed within me? Put your hope in God, for I will yet praise him, my Saviour and my God.
Psalm 42:5 (NIV)

As Christians, it is easy to think that we must not feel despair, be anxious or have fears. We must remain calm and happy; we must always be loving, wise and grateful. We often think that the struggles and burdens we deal with are never a struggle for others. This can make us feel unworthy and alone with our unanswered questions.

However, in those very moments the two of us have encountered a message from *Csendes Percek* – the Hungarian edition of *The Upper Room* – in which someone from another part of the world has written about those same doubts and experiences. *Csendes Percek* is precious to us, because we read stories about real life, not only about 'perfect Christians' and happy endings. We can identify with the feelings of the writers, and sometimes a story completely reflects our own emotions and thoughts. Most of the time we do not receive direct answers or solutions, but we do find compassion.

It is encouraging to know that people living in different cultures and places suffer the burdens of this world just like we do, and they still trust God.

Prayer: *Dear God, we give thanks for opportunities to experience your faithfulness. Thank you for the support you give to us and all our Christian friends around the world. Amen.*

Thought for the day: The experiences of other Christians can encourage me in my struggles.

Sándor and Tenzi Horváth (Tolna County, Hungary)

Grief and anger

Read Isaiah 57:16–19

I have seen his ways, but I will heal him; I will lead him and restore comfort to him and his mourners.
Isaiah 57:18 (ESV)

This year did not start well for me. A very close relative was taken into hospital on New Year's Eve 2023, and he died nine days later. He had been ill for some time but feared a major illness and had stubbornly refused all pleas to seek medical help. The hospital tests showed that there was no major underlying illness, but his body had become too weak to fight a chest infection. The gathered family were asked to give permission for the withdrawal of treatment, as his organs were shutting down.

It was a traumatic and sad situation, but our grief was complicated by anger and frustration at his behaviour. It is possible that depression robbed him of his power to act in time, but unfortunately that inaction has also resulted in major financial and other difficulties for his immediate family.

In the week after his death, as I was wrestling with these conflicting feelings, my morning devotional included the verses above from Isaiah 57 in a version I do not normally use. In most translations, the pronouns are plural and God is speaking about Israel. But here the singular pronouns 'his' and 'him' spoke directly to me of God's presence with the loved one we had lost and gave a promise of healing despite 'his ways'. It gave me hope and comfort in the midst of a bitter loss. Truly 'the word of God is living and active' (Hebrews 4:12).

Prayer: *Lord, help us in times of pain and suffering to hear your word and receive the comfort you wish to give. Amen.*

Thought for the day: God sees me and will restore me.

Mercia Flanagan (Northern Ireland, United Kingdom)

Praying with the nativity

Read Luke 2:1–20
The heavens proclaim [the Lord's] righteousness, and all peoples see his glory.
Psalm 97:6 (NIV)

As the time to take down Christmas decorations drew near, I felt that familiar sadness in my heart. The celebration of Christmas comes and goes so quickly. As I began to remove the pieces of my nativity set, each piece spoke to my heart and prompted me to pray: Lord, help me to be like a shepherd – to lead, nurture and guide those around me to the good shepherd. Lord, help me to be more like the magi – to hear your call and to use the gifts that you have blessed me with to serve others. Lord, help me to be more like Joseph and Mary – to rely on you completely and trust you throughout each day. Lord, help me to be more like Jesus – to show love, kindness, understanding and forgiveness.

Praying with my nativity set in this way helped to ease my post-Christmas sadness and gave me a sense of hope and excitement for the new year and what it would bring. We can look forward with hope when we walk hand in hand with our Lord and Saviour.

Prayer: *Heavenly Father, may the glory and wonder of the nativity lead us through all seasons of the year. Amen.*

Thought for the day: The joy of Christmas can reside in my heart all year long.

Alana C. Broyles (Virginia, USA)

Rejoice and give thanks

Read Ecclesiastes 3:1–8

Give thanks to the Lord, for he is good; his love endures forever.
1 Chronicles 16:34 (NIV)

Since I was a child, I have attended Sunday school. I have always enjoyed it. In my youth, I embraced the opportunity to teach a preteen Sunday school class. For more than 40 years, my calling has been Christian education in different ministry areas of the church.

In July 2022, at 73 years old, I was diagnosed with Alzheimer's disease. I can already feel the effects of the disease. But I have promised, by God's incomparable grace, to continue to be in ministry as long as I am able.

The Lord has blessed me with long life, my family and the fellowship of countless brothers and sisters in the Christian faith. As Ecclesiastes 3:1 reminds us, 'For everything there is a season and a time for every matter under heaven.' God has been my teacher throughout my life, and I will remain grateful to God until the very end.

Prayer: *Generous God, thank you for your many blessings and for giving us opportunities to serve. Lead us into your kingdom. Your will be done. Amen.*

Thought for the day: In all things, I will rejoice and give thanks to God.

Ramonita Rodríguez Sánchez (Puerto Rico)

Peace in the storm

Read Matthew 8:23–27

[Jesus] said to them, 'Why are you afraid, you of little faith?'
Matthew 8:26 (NRSV)

When I was in high school, I travelled back and forth between Germany and the United States by ship several times. Although the vast ocean seemed endless, I had total faith that the captain would bring us safely to the correct destination. Even on stormy nights, the ship stayed on course and safely rolled with the waves.

At times in my life, when it seems like I am being tossed around by waves of uncertainty and hardship, fear causes me to doubt God's plan. But if I could trust the ship's captain, how much more can I trust the creator of the universe? Rather than fear, I want prayer to be my first response to trials. Fear can distract me from God's promise to be with me through every storm.

When a storm developed as the disciples crossed the Sea of Galilee, they were afraid. They begged Jesus to help them, so he calmed the storm. Jesus asked them, 'Why are you afraid, you of little faith?' Even in the face of severe storms, we can trust Jesus to carry us to the destination he has for us. When we surrender ourselves to Jesus, our faith can overcome our fears.

Prayer: *Lord Jesus, help us to remember that you are present with us during life's storms. Give us faith to trust that you will carry us through. Amen.*

Thought for the day: When I face trials, I will choose to trust in the Lord.

John Schliesser (Alabama, USA)

A grateful New Year

Read Psalm 106:1–5

Praise the Lord. Give thanks to the Lord, for he is good; his love endures forever.
Psalm 106:1 (NIV)

I keep an old coffee can on my dining room table. Every day I write something I'm thankful for on a small slip of paper and place it in the can. This discipline of gratitude has become part of my spiritual practice. Sometimes I write down how God has answered a specific prayer request. Other times I record a simple pleasure, such as a phone call with a friend. By New Year's Eve the can is so full I can hardly stuff another piece of paper in!

On New Year's Day I empty the can and read through all these expressions of gratitude. By the time I've gone through all of them, I realise how much God blessed me over the past year. I can look forward to the new year with hope, trusting that God will continue to bless me. I just need to fix my attention on 'whatever is true, whatever is noble, whatever is right, whatever is pure, whatever is lovely, whatever is admirable – if anything is excellent or praiseworthy' (Philippians 4:8).

Prayer: *Gracious God, thank you for a new year and for the blessings of the year that has just passed. We thank you for this new year and trust you will be with us every day. Amen.*

Thought for the day: What will I thank God for today?

Deborah L. Ormay (Pennsylvania, USA)

Small group questions

Wednesday 4 September

1 When have you needed to hold on to others in a physical sense? When have you needed to hold on to others in a metaphorical sense? What were the circumstances?

2 Recall a season when you faced turbulent times and tried to go it alone, without seeking support from God or others. Did you end up seeking support? What was the outcome?

3 Do you struggle to lean on God and others? Why or why not? What helps you accept support and allow others to lift you up? How are you intentional about lifting others up?

4 Why do you think God designed us to need other people? How do you think our inherent need for community impacts our interactions with God and those around us?

5 What can we learn from the relationships Jesus had with his disciples? How do relationships within your church resemble or differ from those between Jesus and the disciples?

Wednesday 11 September

1 Have you ever received comments like those mentioned by today's writer? Have you ever expressed similar sentiments to someone else? Do you find such responses helpful when you are struggling? Why or why not?

2 Do you feel uncomfortable when you are faced with pain, whether it be yours or someone else's? Do you try to move through difficult moments quickly? Why or why not?

3 What happens when you allow yourself to feel grief, pain or anxiety? How is that experience different from when you try to brush aside difficult feelings? What helps you find hope and healing in painful situations?

4 How does scripture encourage you when you are suffering? What scripture verses help you endure painful times? What verses give you hope for the future?

5 When someone tells you they are experiencing something difficult, how do you respond? How do you ensure that you don't minimise their pain? In what ways do you encourage them and remind them that healing will come?

Wednesday 18 September

1 When has a hobby taught you a spiritual truth? What was that truth? How do you ensure that you remain open to unexpected faith lessons in your daily activities?

2 What comes between you and God? Why does this happen? How do you clear away those obstacles and restore your connection with God?

3 How do you know when you are becoming disconnected from God? What changes do you observe in yourself, your relationships and your faith journey in such times?

4 Do you feel grounded in God's grace today? Why or why not? What spiritual practices, prayers or scripture verses ground you and help to cultivate your connection to God?

5 What role does prayer play in your life? How does prayer transform you and your relationship with God? How does prayer connect you with God's grace?

Wednesday 25 September

1 Have you ever been anxious while waiting for news about something or someone? What was the situation? What other emotions did you experience?

2 When you are overcome with worry, what scripture stories most often come to mind? How do those stories help you? What have you learned from them?

3   Do you imagine that it was easy for Jairus to follow Jesus' command to 'just believe'? How do you think you would have responded if you were in Jairus' place?

4   Does fear easily overwhelm you when you are faced with dire news? Why or why not? What helps you to turn your situation over to God and to trust God with the outcome?

5   When your prayers are not answered in the way that you hope, what helps you to remain focused on your relationship with Jesus? How do you remind yourself that Jesus loves you?

Wednesday 2 October

1   When you find yourself overwhelmed with topics to pray about, what do you do? What are your prayers like?

2   Recall a time when you called out to God and received an answer right away. How did the answer change your outlook on prayer?

3   Do you ever worry that your concerns won't be taken care of if you don't pray for them specifically? What verses remind you that God knows and cares for your concerns even if you don't voice them?

4   Is it easy or difficult for you to focus on one thing at a time when you pray? What reminds you to take your time as you pour out your heart to God?

5   How do your prayers change when you trust God's faithfulness and guidance? How does trusting God to answer your prayers affect your faith journey and your relationship with God?

Wednesday 9 October

1 Do you participate in any community outreach programmes? If so, what are they? If not, in what other ways do you contribute to your community?

2 When have you had to go without something that helped you get by financially? What happened? How did you make do without it?

3 Who has cared for you in a time of need? What did they do? How did their kindness and service change your situation or perspective?

4 What gifts and skills has God given you that inspire you to serve others? Where do you see these talents making a difference for others and easing their burdens?

5 What opportunities do you see today to invest in others' lives by serving them? How will you take advantage of those opportunities and show others the love of Christ?

Wednesday 16 October

1 What plant or animal has given you a new perspective on how to persevere in hard times? Why did it give you that perspective?

2 When have you experienced a loss that required you to readjust? What helped you heal from your loss?

3 Why do you think the process of adjusting to loss takes time and looks different for everyone? What are some important lessons that you have learned while healing from loss?

4 What scripture verses encourage you when you are experiencing loss and heartbreak? What verses remind you that God is near?

5 When has God healed your crushed spirit? Who or what did God use to bring about your healing and give you strength? Who in your faith community has recently experienced a loss? What will you do to help them?

Wednesday 23 October

1 What activity has shown you the importance of daily practice? How do your abilities and skills change based on whether you engage in that activity daily?

2 Why do you think consistent practice is important in developing and maintaining skills? Do you find it easy or difficult to practice something consistently? Why?

3 What faith practices do you find most meaningful? Do you practise them daily? How do these practices influence your life and your relationship with God?

4 When have you neglected your faith practices? What caused you to neglect them? What led you back to consistent faith practice?

5 Who in your life encourages you to stay engaged in your faith practice? How does their encouragement help you? How do you encourage others?

Wednesday 30 October

1 Do you relate to the writer of Lamentations in the same way as the author of the meditation? Why or why not? What other scripture writers can you relate to? Why?

2 When you are going through a painful time, do you ever feel hopeless? What scripture passages bring you hope and peace in such times?

3 Recall three instances when God showed you mercy and faithfulness by helping you through a tough situation. How does recalling those times remind you that God will help you through any difficult situation you face?

4 What does it mean to you that you are made strong by the grace of God? What scripture verses, prayers and spiritual practices help you embrace the strength God offers?

5   When are you most aware of God's daily mercy and compassion? How does remembering God's mercy and compassion change the way you respond to challenges?

Wednesday 6 November

1   Recall a time when you were unable to tell where you were going. How did you handle the situation? What happened?

2   Have you ever needed to follow the path in front of you without being able to see clearly? What did this experience teach you about trust?

3   Do you ever find it challenging to know which direction you should take? Why? How do you lean on scripture to find your way in these times?

4   When are you most aware of God's word guiding you? How do you know when you are following God's direction and when you are not?

5   What does it mean to you to be grounded in scripture? What helps you hear God speaking to you through scripture? How does clinging to God's word help you through trials?

Wednesday 13 November

1   Have you or a loved one ever received a frightening diagnosis? How did you respond? What role did your faith play in your response?

2   Do you find it easy or difficult to trust God in all circumstances? Why? When have you tried to tell God how to fix a situation? What was the outcome?

3   Recall a time when you were able to hand over your situation to God and trust God fully. What happened? What helped you release your circumstances to God in this way?

4 When has God offered you peace in a stressful time? How did that peace help you endure? Why do you think God's peace is so transformational?

5 How does trusting God change you? In what ways does trusting God strengthen your faith and alter the way you handle difficult experiences?

Wednesday 20 November

1 When you feel unable to do the work you are called to do, how do you respond? How do you refocus and find ways to serve God despite interruptions and obstacles?

2 Have you ever experienced an interruption that turned out to be an opportunity to serve God? What was the situation? How did that experience change the way you view interruptions?

3 What does Proverbs 16:9 mean to you? Do you find it encouraging or discouraging? How have you found this scripture to be true in your own life?

4 When has God called you to serve in an unpredictable way? How did you answer the call? What happened?

5 Do you tend to be open or closed off to the unexpected ways God wants you to minister? Why? What faith practices help you remain open and willing to serve however God calls you?

Wednesday 27 November

1 Have you ever been in a situation where you were in danger and could not help yourself? What happened? Who helped you get to safety?

2 In what ways have others supported you and helped you through scary situations? How is the outcome different when you have the support of others versus when you don't? Why do you think the support of others is so important?

3 Who in scripture provides the best example of the value of support? Why do you think this is such a good example? What can we learn from this example?

4 When has Jesus found you and offered you supportive guidance? In what ways does Jesus' support differ from the support of other people?

5 In times when you feel isolated, how do you reach out to Jesus and to others? What happens when you reach out? How do you support others who may be feeling isolated?

Wednesday 4 December

1 What does it mean to you to love one another as Jesus loved us? How do you live out this command? How have you witnessed others living it out?

2 When have you received care from someone else? What was it like? What did it teach you about caregiving?

3 When have you witnessed a person laying down their life for another? What happened? How did this sacrifice impact others?

4 When have you shown sacrificial love to someone? What led you to make that sacrifice? How did this experience change the way you relate to and understand Jesus' sacrificial love?

5 Who in your life needs your love and care today? In what ways can you show them sacrificial love?

Wednesday 11 December

1 Why do you think we commonly want to photograph the beautiful sights we encounter? Do you think this prevents us from fully enjoying the present moment? Why or why not?

2 When have you been reminded to stay present and enjoy the moment? What changes within you when you decide to be fully present?

3 Who in your life encourages you to enjoy each moment? How do they do this? In what ways do you see this person being present and grateful?

4 What scripture verses best remind you of the value of each moment? How do these verses encourage you to embrace each day with gratitude?

5 Pause for a moment to reflect on the wonders around you right now. How does taking time to appreciate these wonders inspire gratitude in you?

Wednesday 18 December

1 What Christmas displays bring you the most joy? Do you enjoy the lights and decorations around Christmastime? Why or why not?

2 Have you ever entered the Christmas season with a heavy spirit? What was it like going through the Christmas season feeling this way? Where did you find moments of light despite the heaviness you were experiencing?

3 Who has brought Christ's light to you in a difficult time? What did they do? How did connecting with Christ's light change your situation?

4 What prayers and scripture verses comfort you when you are heavy-hearted? In what ways do these prayers and verses connect you to God and God's light?

5 How will you show others the light of God this Christmas season? Name three ways you can weave God's light through the lives of those in your community this year.

Wednesday 25 December

1 How do you imagine Joseph and Mary felt when Jesus was born? What do you think it might have been like to hear Jesus' first cry?

2 Do you find it easy to forget that Jesus is the most perfect gift? Why or why not? How do you keep Jesus and the gift of salvation at the forefront of your Christmas celebrations?

3 In what ways does God's eternal love for you inspire you to love others? How do you show love to others this time of year and all year round?

4 When did you accept the gift of salvation? How has that gift changed your life?

5 What scripture verses remind you of the value of God's gift of salvation? How can you take time today to thank God for this awesome gift?

Journal page

Become a Friend of BRF Ministries
and give regularly to support our ministry

We help people of all ages to grow in faith

We encourage and support individual Christians and churches as they serve and resource the changing spiritual needs of communities today.

Through **Anna Chaplaincy**
we're enabling churches to provide spiritual care to older people

Through **Living Faith**
we're nurturing faith and resourcing lifelong discipleship

Through **Messy Church**
we're helping churches to reach out to families

Through **Parenting for Faith**
we're supporting parents as they raise their children in the Christian faith

Our ministry is only possible because of the generous support of individuals, churches, trusts and gifts in wills.

As we look to the future and make plans, **regular donations make a huge difference** in ensuring we can both start and finish projects well.

By becoming a Friend and giving regularly to our ministry, you are partnering with us in the gospel and helping change lives.

How your gift makes a difference

£2
a month
Helps us to give away **Living Faith** resources via food banks and chaplaincy services

£10
a month
Helps us to support parents and churches running the **Parenting for Faith** course

£5
a month
Helps us to support **Messy Church** volunteers and grow the wider network

£20
a month
Helps us to develop the reach of **Anna Chaplaincy** and improve spiritual care for older people

How to become a Friend of BRF Ministries

Online – set up a Direct Debit donation at **brf.org.uk/donate** or find out how to set up a Standing Order at **brf.org.uk/friends**

By post – complete and return the form opposite to 'Freepost BRF' (*no other address or stamp is needed*)

If you have any questions, or if you want to change your regular donation or stop giving in the future, do get in touch.

Contact the fundraising team

Email: **giving@brf.org.uk**
Tel: +44 (0)1235 462305
Post: Fundraising team, BRF Ministries,
        15 The Chambers, Vineyard,
        Abingdon OX14 3FE

Registered with

FR

FUNDRAISING
REGULATOR

SHARING OUR VISION – MAKING A GIFT

**I would like to make a donation to support BRF Ministries.
Please use my gift for:**

☐ Where the need is greatest   ☐ Anna Chaplaincy   ☐ Living Faith

☐ Messy Church   ☐ Parenting for Faith

Title	First name/initials	Surname

Address

	Postcode

Email

Telephone

Signature	Date

Our ministry is only possible because of the generous support of individuals, churches, trusts and gifts in wills.

Please treat as Gift Aid donations all qualifying gifts of money made (*tick all that apply*)

giftaid it

☐ today,   ☐ in the past four years,   ☐ and in the future.

I am a UK taxpayer and understand that if I pay less Income Tax and/or Capital Gains Tax in the current tax year than the amount of Gift Aid claimed on all my donations, it is my responsibility to pay any difference.

☐ My donation does not qualify for Gift Aid.

Please notify us if you want to cancel this Gift Aid declaration, change your name or home address, or no longer pay sufficient tax on your income and/or capital gains.

You can also give online at **brf.org.uk/donate**, which reduces our administration costs, making your donation go further.

Please complete other side of this form ➲

SHARING OUR VISION – MAKING A GIFT

Please accept my gift of:

☐ £2 ☐ £5 ☐ £10 ☐ £20 Other £ [   ]

by (*delete as appropriate*):

☐ Cheque/Charity Voucher payable to 'BRF'

☐ MasterCard/Visa/Debit card/Charity card

Name on card

Card no. [   ] [   ] [   ] [   ]

Expires end [M M] [Y Y]   Security code [   ]   Last 3 digits on the reverse of the card

Signature   Date

☐ I would like to leave a gift to BRF Ministries in my will. Please send me further information.

☐ I would like to find out about giving a regular gift to BRF Ministries.

For help or advice regarding making a gift, please contact our fundraising team +44 (0)1865 462305

Your privacy

We will use your personal data to process this transaction. From time to time we may send you information about the work of BRF Ministries that we think may be of interest to you. Our privacy policy is available at **brf.org.uk/privacy**. Please contact us if you wish to discuss your mailing preferences.

Registered with
FUNDRAISING **REGULATOR**

 Please complete other side of this form

Please return this form to 'Freepost BRF'
No other address information or stamp is needed

Bible Reading Fellowship is a charity (233280) and company limited by guarantee (301324), registered in England and Wales

UR0324

God became flesh at Christmas. But how does God, who created all things, live within the limitations of humanity – limitations that humanity itself often resents and tries to transcend? And what does it truly mean to be human? As contemporary society grapples with questions of identity, justice and medical ethics, *Embracing Humanity* deftly explores how different aspects of being human are both inhabited and transformed in the incarnation.

BRF Advent Book: Embracing Humanity
A journey towards becoming flesh
Isabelle Hamley
with a foreword by the Archbishop of Canterbury
978 1 80039 226 7 £9.99
brfonline.org.uk

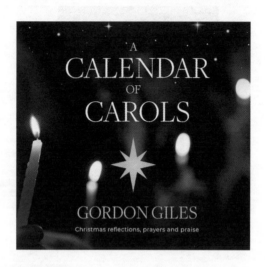

Christmas is a musical destination as well as a spiritual one, yet when we reach the newborn Christ child in the manger, what do we see? What music do we hear in our hearts as we join our songs with those of the angels? In 25 short chapters, each concluding with a specially written prayer, Gordon Giles explores the spiritual and biblical allusions to be found within our best-loved Christmas carols. *A Calendar of Carols* can be used either as an Advent calendar up to Christmas, or more flexibly over the Christmas season and into January.

A Calendar of Carols
Christmas reflections, prayers and praise
Gordon Giles
978 1 80039 279 3 £9.99
brfonline.org.uk

How to encourage Bible reading in your church

BRF Ministries has been helping individuals connect with the Bible for over 100 years. We want to support churches as they seek to encourage church members into regular Bible reading.

Order a Bible reading resources pack
This pack is designed to give your church the tools to publicise our Bible reading notes. It includes:

- Sample Bible reading notes for your congregation to try.
- Publicity resources, including a poster.
- A church magazine feature about Bible reading notes.

The pack is free, but we welcome a £5 donation to cover the cost of postage. If you require a pack to be sent outside the UK or require a specific number of sample Bible reading notes, please contact us for postage costs. For more information about what the current pack contains, go to **brfonline.org.uk/pages/bible-reading-resources-pack**.

How to order and find out more
- Email **enquiries@brf.org.uk**
- Phone us on +44 (0)1865 319700 Mon–Fri 9.30–17.00.
- Write to us at BRF Ministries, 15 The Chambers, Vineyard, Abingdon OX14 3FE.

Keep informed about our latest initiatives
We are continuing to develop resources to help churches encourage people into regular Bible reading, wherever they are on their journey. Join our email list at **brfonline.org.uk/signup** to stay informed about the latest initiatives that your church could benefit from.

Subscriptions

The Upper Room is published in January, May and September.

Individual subscriptions
The subscription rate for orders for 4 or fewer copies includes postage and packing:

The Upper Room annual individual subscription   £19.50

Group subscriptions
Orders for 5 copies or more, sent to ONE address, are post free:
The Upper Room annual group subscription   £14.97

Please do not send payment with order for a group subscription. We will send an invoice with your first order.

Please note that the annual billing period for group subscriptions runs from 1 May to 30 April.

Copies of the notes may also be obtained from Christian bookshops.

Single copies of *The Upper Room* cost £4.99.

Prices valid until 30 April 2025.

Giant print version
The Upper Room is available in giant print for the visually impaired, from:

Torch Trust for the Blind
Torch House
Torch Way
Northampton Road
Market Harborough   Tel: +44 (0)1858 438260
LE16 9HL   **torchtrust.org**

> **All our Bible reading notes can be ordered online by visiting brfonline.org.uk/subscriptions**

☐ I would like to take out a subscription myself (complete your name and address details once)

☐ I would like to give a gift subscription (please provide both names and addresses)

Title .... First name/initials .... Surname ....

Address ....

.... Postcode ....

Telephone .... Email ....

Gift subscription name ....

Gift subscription address ....

.... Postcode ....

Gift message (20 words max. or include your own gift card):

....

....

Please send *The Upper Room* beginning with the January 2025 / May 2025 / September 2025 issue (*delete as appropriate*):

Annual individual subscription ☐ £19.50

Optional donation* to support the work of BRF Ministries £ ....

Total enclosed £ .... (cheques should be made payable to 'BRF')

*Please complete and return the Gift Aid declaration on page 159 to make your donation even more valuable to us.

Method of payment

Please charge my MasterCard / Visa with £ ....

Card no. ☐☐☐☐ ☐☐☐☐ ☐☐☐☐ ☐☐☐☐

Expires end ☐☐ ☐☐   Security code ☐☐☐   Last 3 digits on the reverse of the card

THE UPPER ROOM: GROUP SUBSCRIPTION FORM

All our Bible reading notes can be ordered online by visiting brfonline.org.uk/subscriptions

❑ Please send me .... copies of *The Upper Room* January 2025 / May 2025 / September 2025 issue (*delete as appropriate*)

Title .... First name/initials .... Surname ....

Address ....

.... Postcode ....

Telephone .... Email ....

Please do not send payment with this order. We will send an invoice with your first order.

Christian bookshops: All good Christian bookshops stock our resources. For your nearest stockist, please contact us.

Telephone: The BRF office is open Mon–Fri 9.30–17.00. To place your order, telephone +44 (0)1865 319700.

Online: brfonline.org.uk/group-subscriptions

❑ Please send me a Bible reading resources pack to encourage Bible reading in my church

Please return this form with the appropriate payment to:
BRF Ministries, 15 The Chambers, Vineyard, Abingdon OX14 3FE

For terms and cancellation information, please visit **brfonline.org.uk/terms**.

Bible Reading Fellowship is a charity (233280) and company limited by guarantee (301324), registered in England and Wales

UR0324

To order

Online: **brfonline.org.uk**
Telephone: +44 (0)1865 319700 Mon–Fri 9.30–17.00

Delivery times within the UK are normally 15 working days. Prices are correct at the time of going to press but may change without prior notice.

Title	Price	Qty	Total
Embracing Humanity	£9.99		
A Calendar of Carols	£9.99		

POSTAGE AND PACKING CHARGES			
Order value	UK	Europe	Rest of world
Under £7.00	£2.00	Available on request	Available on request
£7.00–£29.99	£3.00		
£30.00 and over	FREE		

Total value of books	
Postage and packing	
Donation*	
Total for this order	

* Please complete the Gift Aid declaration below

Please complete in BLOCK CAPITALS

Title .... First name/initials .... Surname...............................

Address ....

.... Postcode ....

Acc. No. .... Telephone ....

Email ....

Gift Aid Declaration

gift aid it

Please treat as Gift Aid donations all qualifying gifts of money made (*tick all that apply*)

☐ today, ☐ in the past four years, ☐ and in the future **or** ☐ My donation does not qualify for Gift Aid.

I am a UK taxpayer and understand that if I pay less Income Tax and/or Capital Gains Tax in the current tax year than the amount of Gift Aid claimed on all my donations, it is my responsibility to pay any difference.

Please notify BRF Ministries if you want to cancel this declaration, change your name or home address, or no longer pay sufficient tax on your income and/or capital gains.

Method of payment

☐ Cheque (made payable to BRF) ☐ MasterCard / Visa

Card no. ☐☐☐☐ ☐☐☐☐ ☐☐☐☐ ☐☐☐☐

Expires end ☐M ☐M ☐Y ☐Y   Security code ☐☐☐   Last 3 digits on the reverse of the card

Please return this form to:

BRF Ministries, 15 The Chambers, Vineyard, Abingdon OX14 3FE | **enquiries@brf.org.uk**
For terms and cancellation information, please visit **brfonline.org.uk/terms**.

BRF Ministries

Inspiring people of all ages to grow in Christian faith

BRF Ministries is the home of Anna Chaplaincy, Living Faith, Messy Church and Parenting for Faith

As a charity, our work would not be possible without fundraising and gifts in wills.
To find out more and to donate,
visit brf.org.uk/give or call +44 (0)1235 462305